Inside Outside

Inside Outside

Six short plays by
SONALI BHATTACHARYYA
DEBORAH BRUCE
ZOE COOPER
KALUNGI SSEBANDEKE
JOEL TAN
JOE WHITE

NICK HERN BOOKS

London

www.nickhernbooks.co.uk

A Nick Hern Book

Inside/Outside first published in Great Britain in 2021 as a paperback original by Nick Hern Books Limited, The Glasshouse, 49a Goldhawk Road, London W12 8QP, in association with the Orange Tree Theatre

Designed and typeset by Nick Hern Books, London
Printed in the UK by Mimeo Ltd, Huntingdon, Cambridgeshire PE29 6XX

A CIP catalogue record for this book is available from the British Library

ISBN 978 1 83904 001 6

Contents

Introduction

Guy Jones

As I write, the Orange Tree Theatre has been closed for a year. It's time to switch the lights back on. *Inside/Outside* will be the first time we have told stories here since March 2020.

It feels important that we reopen with new plays – by writers who have been an important part of the Orange Tree's story over the last few years, and to new writers who we are excited to introduce to audiences. I've been thinking back to how these playwrights came into our lives. Together, they tell a story about how the Orange Tree has made its name as a home for new plays.

Deborah Bruce's *The Distance* was the first new play in artistic director Paul Miller's inaugural season at the Orange Tree in 2014. I remember Paul sending it to me with that sense of glee – finding an excellent new play can be like finding treasure. I read it in a Costa Coffee in Finchley, and marvelled at how Deborah used the play to ask difficult questions about motherhood, with such humour. I replied to Paul immediately – we had to see if we could do it. We did, and it was an immediate success.

We met Zoe Cooper in the Attenborough Room at the theatre, where so many of our ideas start out, drinking tea from ugly cups. The team had fallen in love with *Jess and Joe Forever* in one of our script meetings, and we couldn't wait to talk about it. Zoe's plays tell stories of queer people with warmth and inclusivity, with actors turning out to the audience and welcoming them into their worlds. In both *Jess and Joe Forever* and *Out of Water* she is concerned by the world we are passing on to the next generation. The impact of the virus on young people is immeasurable, and so I'm glad that in Zoe's play *The Kiss*, and in Sonali Bhattacharyya's *Two Billion Beats*, we create the space to think about the world we want them to grow up in, and the role grown-ups might play in shaping that.

Both Sonali and Joe White are graduates of the OT's Writers Collective programme. The Collective has been a key part of the theatre's offer to the playwriting community: we meet in the rehearsal room amidst unwashed-up mugs from the day's rehearsal, and spark collaborations and conversations as we explore new ideas for the theatre.

Sonali went on to be the OT's Writer on Attachment through the Channel 4 Playwrights' Scheme in 2018, and it was a treat to work with her during that year. As the world becomes a harder place to live, Sonali's work combines political energy with optimism for the human spirit, and that is just what we need now.

After his time on the Collective, we produced Joe White's play *Mayfly*, and the production remains a favourite amongst our audiences. The characters in Joe's plays aren't used to being given the microphone – lost souls in search of connection, often erased from the national story because of accidents of class or geography.

Kalungi Ssebandeke and Joel Tan are writers new to the Orange Tree. Kalungi came into our lives when he was cast in our production of *Blood Knot* in 2019. It was clear to everyone that here was a fantastic actor, and one day between a matinee and an evening show we sat down for a chat and he pushed a fascinating play about the boxer Bill Richmond across the table (or at least into my inbox).

I first heard about Joel when his epic and shape-shifting play *Love in the Time of the Ancients* was nominated for an award run by the tireless champions of new work, Papatango Theatre Company. Joel had been putting down roots in the London playwriting scene having arrived here from Singapore. He came in for a meeting at the Orange Tree shortly before the world shut down, and optimistic conversations about what we might be able to do evaporated. So it feels right that with Kalungi and Joel we can pick up where we left off, championing the work of new talent.

*

The threshold between the inside and the outside has felt particularly impermeable over this last year, as we have been asked to stay in our homes. We have also been particularly attuned to the way the shifting weather outside our windows has affected our ability to ride this storm: 'Now the sun is here, I am all-powerful,' said one of the directors to me during a script meeting a few weeks ago, with her face bathed in sunlight.

As we Zoomed one another during the winter lockdown at the end of 2020, 'in' and 'out' felt like an appropriate axis by which to examine the world we inhabit now, anticipating a time when our freedoms might return.

The *Inside/Outside* plays also remind us that we can't take those freedoms for granted, and that the victims of this year are many. Homelessness is on the rise,
loneliness is deadly,
the monster of racism lurks in everyday interactions, and is far from being weeded out,
the pandemic has put families and relationships under enormous strain
and many of the inequalities we live with are written into the systems in which we are asked to participate.

But the plays also offer hope. Two strangers learn that they can help one another move forwards in Joe White's *Ursa Major*, and in Zoe Cooper's *The Kiss*, Lou is changed by the time she has lived through, but still committed to how she might pave the way for a new generation. Like Meg in Joel Tan's play, we are looking forward to when the daffodils come, and we can once again tell one another stories, breathe the same air, embrace.

March 2021

Inside

Inside was first performed and livestreamed from the Orange Tree Theatre, Richmond, on 25 March 2021. The cast and creative team were as follows:

Guidesky and I	by Deborah Bruce
DIANA	Samantha Spiro
When the Daffodils	by Joel Tan
MEG	Ishia Bennison
SAMIA	Jessica Murrain
Ursa Major	by Joe White
JAY	Fisayo Akinade
CALLISTO	Sasha Winslow
Director	Anna Himali Howard
Designer	Shankho Chaudhuri
Lighting Designer	Jessica Hung Han Yun
Sound Designer & Composer	Anna Clock
Casting	Sarah Murray
Company Stage Manager	Jenny Skivens
Stage Manager	Caoimhe Regan

The *Inside/Outside* series of plays was curated by Guy Jones, Orange Tree Literary Associate

Guidesky and I

Deborah Bruce

Characters

DIANA, *late fifties/early sixties*
Young MAN
Older MAN

1.

DIANA *has her coat on, a tote bag of piano sheet music over her shoulder, a large road atlas under her arm. She's holding a fan heater and a flattened blue cat cave.*

DIANA.

Dear Guidesky125,

The cat cave has arrived.

This IS NOT what I ordered.

I ordered a heather-grey merino-wool cat cave and I have received a blue synthetic thing in two – flimsy parts – with a, shoddily attached zip joining the two parts together.

You need to send me a REFUND IMMEDIATELY

please.

Yours Sincerely,

Diana Harris Ms.

Pause.

When will they reply, do we think? How long do these things take?

Can you get a refund straight back into your bank account if you paid for something on PayPal?

Maybe I should send an email to PayPal.

Such an idiot.

Why can't I *do* things.

DIANA *wants to put the cat cave down but doesn't know where to put it.*

She remembers the fan heater.

Oh. Now. Does this work?

She is looking around for a plug socket, she finds one and plugs it in.

It blows heat at her and smells bad.

Yes it does.

She lets it fan-heat for a few moments to make sure.

Good.

She unplugs it, picks it up.

She's flustered.

FAO Guidesky125

Hello.

This is Diana Harris again.
Just to amend my previous email.

I will also be taking this up with PayPal having looked at the comments on your website and realised that this is what you do! Take decent people's money and send them something cheap and nasty when they ordered a – high quality product in good faith. Goodness me!
What a – way to behave.
I wonder if you feel ashamed of yourself?

Pause.

I demand a refund.

Of the full amount you fraudulently took from me.

Immediately.

Yours Sincerely

Diana Harris. Ms.

Pause.

Should I leave some lights on, make the place look lived in?

I haven't a clue when I'll be back.

2.

DIANA *is seated*.

That's six roadkill on the A3, mostly foxes, a badger.
Some poor thing that looks like a German shepherd but can't
be, surely.

It's more trafficky than usual.

(*Mock/playful shouting out*.) Where are you all going?
You're not supposed to be going anywhere!

They're probably looking at me thinking the same!

Don't worry! I'm only moving between my little flat in
Chiswick and my mother's house in Brookwood not seeing a
single soul in between so don't worry about me, I'm not
spreading the virus.

I'm just going to jump out of the car when I get there
run straight into the house
lock the door behind me.

What about unloading the boot?
That can wait.

Not a single soul.

I have an underlying feeling of unease.

I used to sing along to songs!

(*Sings out*.) They say no no it won't last forever!

(*Quietly, to herself*.) I just took a trip on my love for him.

Think of normal things. Stop imagining a dead cat.
Not Misty, a ginger one.
With its whiskers frayed, its claws snapped. There's blood
trickling out of its nose.
Hit by a car most probably.

Why am I thinking about that?
I don't even *know* a ginger cat.

3.

DIANA *is standing in her coat, holding several bags.*

Well it looks the same.

No reason for it not to.

In you go then.

Here we are.

She stands without speaking for a while, looking round the space.

Dear me.
Piles and layers.
All covered in dust.

Should have brought some, there'll be plenty here.
Dusters.
Dust pan and brush on the arm of the chair,
she'll have been sweeping out the hearth.

She'll have been kneeling down to sweep it.
You can get dizzy if you stand up too fast.

I've got my work cut out here then.
I'm going to be working my socks off with this lot.

Good thinking to bring the fan heater, it's cold through to the brick.

She snaps into action, puts her bags down, takes off her scarf and coat.

Gillian's daughter has overfed Misty. Biscuits under the rim of the plate – spilled out everywhere.
There's a biscuit, all the way over there on the floor, by the sink.
She's written a note – with her left hand it looks like.
'Dianna', double 'N', 'If – *something* – let us know.'
I can't read that.
I've forgotten my other glasses.
Damn.

Left useless on my bedside table, next to my pills, lit by the
light seeping in from the hall – why did I leave the *hall* light on,
who sits in the hall in their own home all night, no one. What a
chump.
If someone breaks in I won't be surprised. I'll deserve it.

Well this Wi-Fi is bad and slow.

What if they've said something about the cat cave and I need to
say something back?

The floor's sticky.
The fridge smells of off.
She hated waste.
That map needs folding back into its cover.
Where do I start?

Have I stepped into someone else's body leaning on a kitchen
counter waiting for a kettle?

'Do you want a hottie?'

I don't mind *Come Dine with Me*.
I've seen this one before but I can't remember who wins the
money.
I'm suspicious of everyone,
people only think of themselves.

Everyone signed my 'Sorry to Hear You're Leaving' card, even
Head Office,
and they knew I'd been there the longest and it wasn't fair.

That banging sound.
It's the wind making the plastic sheeting on next door's roof
slap against their scaffolding.
Did I lock the car?
It's pitch black out there like the deep inside of a head.

I want to tell someone that I'm here, who should I tell?

'I've arrived safely.'

'I'll probably be here for a few days.'

Yes I'm here get used to it.
No point gawping at me, miaowing.
I thought cats were supposed to sit on laps.

I saw a YouTube video of a lady wrapping her cat in a towel and sort of bundling it in a box.
I bought you a bed!

I saw it poking out of the envelope, what's this? That's not merino wool.
It's not what I ordered, they *know* it's not. There's no picture of it on the website. You can't click on it by mistake.
They lured me in.
All the nonsense of choosing the different colours.
They saw me coming.
Merino wool's supposed to be warmer than alpaca that's why I chose it
why didn't I read the reviews?
Too late now so more fool me.

All the things that need doing here.

The sheets will be damp I expect.

Lucky Sal in Australia!
Lucky her there's a travel ban!
Good excuse not to have to clear out a house.

4.

Empty stage.
Distant sound of the piano being played somewhere in the house.
After a while it stops mid-tune, the music left hanging.

5.

DIANA *holds a piece of toast and seems distracted.*

Should I keep the calendar? Put it in the car and drive it back to
my flat.
Her handwriting up to August.
The back of the empty pages I could use for scrap paper.
I should keep it to treasure and remember. She had the same one
every year. What is it about perforated edges, I used to beg to be
the one to tear them as a child.

Throw it away. For God's sake! A plain calendar! Not even
pictures, just.
Plain old. What's wrong with you?
Come along now.
Lots to do.

I'd rather not drive to the dump in the dark.

The doorbell rings.

DIANA *stands completely still.*
Waits.

Where's my mask? In a pocket. It's safer not to answer.

Someone bringing me something home-made. Forcing me to be
grateful so they can be kind, I know that dance.

People never stand two metres away anyway

goodness look how the skin on my hands is chapped.
Chapped hands warm heart.

Are they still there?

Go. Go. Go.

They've gone.

Too many clocks in this house, listen tick tick tick it's an
infestation.

6.

DIANA *stands with her car keys in her hand and a bag-for-life full of Tupperware at her feet.*

'Dear Customer
Thank you for your purchase. We are so sorry to hear that.
Don't worry, we will try our best to solve this out for you.
To save time and effort of customers and us we would like to
offer you a three-pound refund as compensation. Due to the cost
of returning postage, which is not worth it to return it back to
us. For any other inquiries, please feel free to contact us. Kind
Regards, Guidesky125.'

No!

Absolutely no!
I don't want what you sent me! I didn't order that!
You WILFULLY.
You KNOWINGLY.
You SENT ME SOMETHING I DID NOT ORDER.
On PURPOSE.
I
I will NOT.
NOT a three-pound refund. A FULL refund. The FULL amount.

She contains herself.

Give me a full refund straight away or I will escalate my action
to the next level. Yours Sincerely Diana Harris Ms.

PS Don't think you can get away with this because you can't.

Pause.

7.

DIANA *peering, squinting, under her breath*

Guidesky
Guidesky125
Fraud account
Beware. Scam.
Useless without my glasses!
Buyer beware! Guidesky125, also operating as Mitinight and
Bluebird21 these too are fraud accounts – This is a fraudulent
website.
Do not order – Suspected scam.
Why has this happened to me?
Stupid stupid idiot.
What's done is done.
No point getting upset about something you can't change.
When you feel it closing in
you know what to do, get busy.
Find
something
to do.

Right.
Well.

There's lots to do.

Here we go.
What about all the linen napkins, iron them or charity shop?
Iron them or charity shop, what do we think?
Iron what? Oh yes, the napkins.
Do people use napkins these days, for big family gatherings of
course, so.
What do *I* want with them?
Saved to spite me,
mentioned every visit.
Her pretending to forget I had no mouths to dab at.
Tea towels.

No one irons a tea towel!
Just to be
Just to be scrunched up and
left on a
stuffed in a
–

Hello.

An image has slipped into the frame of my mind from a place.

Bare legs –
The hem of my summer dress –
The boy I loved.
My heart dropped from a great height.

Four hands on the piano keys.
Dust on his sleeve from falling off the rope swing.
The waistcoat he wore
the day he said he'd be back that never came.

From napkins and tea towels to –

Attached to nothing!
How thoughts come!
From nowhere.

DIANA *looks around the space.*

Will I unravel in this house?

She gathers some things into a bag.
She holds a Tupperware and a mismatched lid.

8.

A torch switches on.
DIANA *is in her nightdress.*
It's the middle of the night.

'Dear Diana Harris
If you want all refund, you should return the item you received
only then we will refund you, this whole process can last two or
three months and maybe the return parcel is lost in transit, so
you will not receive any refund or item. A three-pound refund is
the best choice for you. We highly recommend you to accept
our offer. Three pounds is the maximum value we can offer to
refund to you on this case. Please understand. Kind Regards,
Guidesky125.'

DIANA *stands still for several moments taking this in.*

You're thinking, oh she won't have the energy, she won't have
the patience to pursue this, she'll give up, she'll resign herself
to the loss of a few pounds, twenty-three pounds, she'll get fed
up of this. This back and forth, this email tennis.
I know what you want to happen.
She'll run out of steam, leave it for a day or two, forget to come
back to it.
I won't.
I see you, Guidesky125.
Where did you get those pictures of a woman weaving? The
detail of the natural dyes, the merino wool,
you drew me in.
You were cruising around the streets of the internet in a car with
blacked-out windows waiting for me to cross your path.
I trusted you,
sent you my mother's money and you sent me a, pig's ear,
that I would never have –
no one would have ordered it!
And now you refuse to refund me, oh, it's not worth it, it's not
worth the trouble
but it *is* worth it.

It very much is worth it because –
Because
Your business is built on deceit and you spread distrust like a
virus.
If you add up each of our single contributions to the world, add
them up, what are they worth?
However tiny, because this is just a tiny –
It's all the world is!
The accumulation of tiny interactions. We *live* in them.

I haven't seen a single soul for nearly one hundred days –
my mother died alone –
and you can't complete an honest small transaction with a
stranger on the internet?
Listen to me, Guidesky, I want my money back.
And if you don't give me my money back I am going to –

I'm going to –

To –

I'm going to kill you, Guidesky. I'm going to find you and I'm
going to –
kill you.

DIANA *stands quiet for a moment.*

Yours Sincerely Diana Harris Ms.

She feels a bit foolish.
She feels a bit upset.
She switches off the torch and stays in the dark for a moment.

(*Very quiet under her breath.*) Live each day as if it were your
last live each day as if it were your last.

After a while she's lit by a blue fridge light.
She is in a different part of the space and holding a plate with
half a Scotch egg on.
She eats the Scotch egg.

9.

DIANA *is seated, she has a blanket round her shoulders, a
clock ticks.*
She has the blue synthetic cat cave in her lap.

Who have I spoken to since she died? Who?
Come on, there must be – this is ridiculous.
I go to Costcutters, don't I?
I see the lady there, she's there every day, *very* friendly, says
'Hello!' she can't believe how long it's gone on, she's getting
sick of this now!
Her cardigan covers her name badge, it ends in 'ta'.
Ri-ta, Gee-ta, Si-ta
she's not a *friend*,
but she's friendly,
it's a lift.
It's a 'spring in your step'.
Who else.
I said a message on Carolyn's answerphone,
it was the voice the machine comes with – she can't come to the
phone – promises you nothing. Who knows what's really
happening? She could be standing there, listening to hear who it
is. Not her.
Is that it.
Next door,
upstairs,
two doors along –
Opposite are nice. Opposite posted a note through my door
about children selling cupcakes on a stall.
I didn't go over. I should have done. There you see, examples of
opportunities I could take but choose not to, that's better. It's
not as if there are no opportunities to take.
There's an area to improve on.
When I'm back home, if it happens again, I'll go!
Buy a cupcake! I can always throw it away without the children
seeing me.
What else?

I would sit in a café or restaurant by myself, I'm more than happy to do that.
Are you using this chair? Can I take this chair?
Yes of course! Go ahead! Move my bag. Very friendly, very positive interaction. Thank you. Thank you you're welcome, have a lovely day.
It makes you,
feel something.

I saw that couple again a few weeks later, walking.

I'm really very fortunate. To live in a community.
A very friendly.
And civilised.

DIANA *zips the two pieces of the cat cave together and sets it on the floor.*

It's not too bad. Misty!

What do you care what it's made of! What colour it is!

Cats sleep for twenty hours out of twenty-four or something.
Alright for some!
Misty!

Pause.

She's gone off somewhere.

She stands and changes position.

No new emails.

What if Guidesky's not the head honcho but just a young man or a boy or a,
someone who had nothing to do with the scam – nothing to do with the fraudulent –
The business side of things.
What if it's not his fault, he doesn't make the decisions, he just does as he's told. Packs up the cheap blue caves. Doesn't know you haven't ordered it. No idea which person has ordered what.

What if Guidesky is just an innocent in all of this.

He's poorly paid, his working conditions are ropey, no health and safety.

Guidesky's not even his name, is it.

No one cares what his name is.

They call him 'You!'

'Hey!'

'Get over here!'

I won't sleep now thinking about this.
I'll lie there all night in a muffle

see a young boy's small hands scrabbling to fix a zip

his chapped hands

or my chapped hands?

In the half-sleep –
imagine a house flooded,
Mum's precious things spoiled
bobbing around in dirty dishwater
lapping at my ankles.

Nights are twice as long as days.

I'll have a walk!
Hat. Coat.
I'm going round in circles here!

If there's no reply on the computer when I get in I'll go back out –
I can't be in this house with the hollow empty internet tube pumping silence into the walls and floors.

I used to have other people
cardigans over the backs of chairs
where did they –
where did they go?

Guidesky.
Guidesky125.

I haven't made you up, have I?
You wrote to me
didn't you?

10.

Early morning. Birdsong.
DIANA *stands looking out.*
Blanket still on her shoulders.
She hasn't slept.

Whatever happened to the rope swing?
Some father flung the rope over –
a locked knot to stand or sit on, standing was scarier
you had to, *push* with your buttocks, sort of *launch* yourself
forwards ram yourself hard into empty space and air
you'd get dragged back and
tighten and launch, tighten and launch until momentum took
you –
it was effortless for a swing, or two swings
until you slowed down
scuffed your feet into the dust to stop
then it was someone else's turn but
every second was worth it and you queued up to go again.

Is the rope still on the tree, I wonder?

There's a knock on the door.

DIANA *doesn't react to it.*

It'll be slimy with moss. Frayed to a thread probably.
Or just not there at all.
Weathered into absence.
–
Loss is a deep pool you can't just dip your toe into.

There's another knock.

DIANA *makes eye contact with the audience and rolls her eyes and shakes her head.*

They'll go away – people always do.

A young MAN *steps into the space.*
He wears a pair of corduroy trousers and a waistcoat and a jacket.
He looks around the space.
He takes off his jacket and hangs it up.

He has a name badge that says 'GUIDESKY125'.

DIANA *turns to face him.*
She looks at him a long time.

MAN. Hello.

DIANA. Oh, hello.

> *They are a bit awkward, sheepish.*
> *Like two socially awkward people,* DIANA *more so.*

MAN. How are you?

DIANA. What are you here for?

MAN. Oh yeah, I have something for you.

DIANA. What is it?

MAN. Do you know what it is?

DIANA. No, I just said, what is it?

MAN. What do you think it is?

DIANA. I don't know.

MAN. Guess.

> *Pause.*

DIANA. A cat cave?

> *The* MAN *exits.*

> DIANA *stands very still.*

She briefly glances at someone in the audience,
embarrassed.

The MAN *returns, he is in the exact same clothes and badge*
but he is played by an actor thirty years older.
He is holding a merino-wool cat cave.
He holds it out to DIANA, *she takes it.*

DIANA. Thank you.

MAN. Is it what you ordered?

DIANA. Yes I think so yes.

The MAN *remains standing there.*

MAN. I need to, take the other one back.

DIANA. Oh right.

DIANA *looks over to the blue synthetic cat cave on the floor.*

Oh.

The cat's, in it.
I didn't think she'd –

MAN. That's okay.

DIANA. I didn't think she'd like it.

MAN. It's okay.

The MAN *puts his jacket back on.*
DIANA *hands him back the merino-wool cat cave.*

DIANA. I'll probably just finish up here.

I might tidy up that puzzle – put it back in the box.

I expect I'll head back to my flat on Sunday evening. Or
Monday.

DIANA *does a little laugh.*

MAN. Okay.
Can I play the piano before I go?

DIANA. If you like.

MAN. Okay.
  Goodbye.

DIANA. Goodbye.

The MAN *sits down in the audience.*

DIANA *is self-conscious under our gaze.*

DIANA. Right.

  Let's press on.

DIANA *looks around for a job to do.*

There is the sound of someone playing the piano from another room in the house.

DIANA *stops.*

Listens.

Lights fade to black.

The End.

When the Daffodils

Joel Tan

Characters

MEG, *late sixties or older*
SAMIA, *early thirties*

Winter. The sun sets over the course of the play.

Inside. The living room of a small single flat. Two chairs, a table, on which is a radio, playing Christmas tunes.

MEG, *elderly, in a Christmas jumper, sits in an armchair, staring out the window. She hums along. The Christmas tunes are suddenly interrupted. A message or report of some sort, public in nature, but scrambled, unintelligible. MEG is unfazed by it. It finishes. The Christmas tunes resume.*

The doorbell.

MEG *gets up, excited.*

SAMIA *enters in a big overcoat and a face mask. She's got a backpack, and is carrying paper bags of groceries. She sets them down on a table. She takes off her face mask. MEG turns off the tunes.*

MEG. You needn't have rung, I'm not expecting anyone else.

SAMIA. Merry Christmas, Meg.

MEG. And you.

SAMIA. Always good to ring, you never know.

MEG. Know what?

SAMIA. You might have been naked, or –

MEG. Naked!

SAMIA. Or with company.

MEG. Company!

SAMIA. Why'd you turn off the music?

MEG. Oh, did you –

SAMIA. Yeah!

MEG. I just thought – you don't, your family don't, celebrate Christmas do they, Samia?

SAMIA. That's very considerate of you, Meg, but we'll be fine. Not like they aren't playing Jesus songs everywhere you go now.

MEG. Oh they're back on that, are they?

SAMIA. Used to hate it, but you take what you can nowadays, hey?

MEG. Keeps spirits up, as you say.

SAMIA (*pulling a packet of sprouts out of the bag*). Yeah, helps sell Brussels sprouts too.

MEG. Oh you got them!

SAMIA. Couldn't find them on the stalk, but –

MEG. Oh that's perfect.

SAMIA. I'll let you sort through it all, yeah? I threw something extra in there…

MEG (*rifling through*). Extra… (*Producing chocolates.*) oh you've been naughty.

SAMIA. Cognac centres.

MEG. Oh yummy.

SAMIA (*starting to fuss with her mask*). Really shouldn't have, what with your diabetes and all that, but it's the holidays, isn't it?

MEG. Oh Samia, don't go. Stay a little longer today.

SAMIA. Stay –

MEG. I know I'm at the end of your route and –

SAMIA. Yeah.

MEG. And you're not too far off, and I – you do drink, don't you?

SAMIA. I do, yeah.

MEG. Made some mulled wine.

SAMIA. Yeah?

MEG. With all the trimmings.

SAMIA. And what would those be?

MEG. Vanilla, bit of allspice.

SAMIA. Can't say no to that.

MEG. You're staying!

MEG *goes off into the kitchen.*

SAMIA (*calling off*). Not too much, though, Meg.

SAMIA *stands uneasily in the space. She takes off her overcoat. Reveals a government uniform of some sort.* MEG *returns with two mugs.*

MEG. I got you a biscuit too.

SAMIA. You spoil me, Meg.

MEG. Merry Christmas.

SAMIA. Merry Christmas.

MEG. And you know what?

SAMIA. What?

MEG (*meaning the chocolates*). Should we be cheeky?

SAMIA. Go on then.

MEG *breaks out the chocolates.*

They sit, contentedly, MEG *squealing as she pops a chocolate.*

MEG. At the risk of sounding too optimistic, any big plans tonight?

SAMIA. I dunno. Yeah. Just me and my girlfriend.

MEG. Letty.

SAMIA. Letty, yeah.

MEG. And the dog.

SAMIA. Hester.

MEG. Hester, yes. Odd name for a dog, Hester.

SAMIA. So yeah, just us three, really. TV. Chinese food. Oh. Wait. Forgot. I saw something at the shop and thought of you. (*Retrieving a present from her bag.*) We're not meant to get our charges presents, but I do have my soft spots. Merry Christmas.

MEG. Oh, Merry Christmas love. Thank you.

SAMIA. Open it.

MEG *opens it. It's a calendar.*

MEG. Oh it's precious.

SAMIA. It's the cats, isn't it, they're so cute, they crack me up.

MEG. They're adorable. (*Getting up and clearing some space on the table.*) I'll put it right here.

SAMIA. I figured since I won't be around for New Year's…

MEG. Where're you going?

SAMIA. Oh, not travelling, no, nowhere, I've got the week off is all. You might see the fireworks from this window, I reckon. Meg?

MEG *holds the calendar in her hand, puzzled.*

What is it?

MEG. Nothing.

SAMIA. Don't you like it?

MEG. I do, it's just.

SAMIA. What?

MEG. The dates are funny, aren't they?

SAMIA. The dates?

MEG. Not the right year, is it? Am I seeing things?

SAMIA. What?

MEG. They've got the year wrong, haven't they? It's for this year.

SAMIA. Don't be ridiculous.

MEG. Not ridiculous! Come see –

SAMIA. Why would I get you the...

Pause.

MEG. No you're right.

SAMIA. You okay, Meg? You're –

MEG. Elder moment. God, that's embarrassing.

SAMIA. Nothing to be embarrassed about, Meg. You've already snuck a couple mulled wines in today, haven't you?

MEG (*hugging* SAMIA). I'm so happy to see you on this special, holy day. Sorry they're making you work Christmas.

SAMIA. This is nothing, Meg, I enjoy it.

MEG. That's good.

SAMIA. Like seeing friends, really.

MEG. It's very good of you.

SAMIA. Well don't shout home too much, Meg.

MEG. No?

SAMIA. Still a job, isn't it.

MEG. Not just a job. It's Christian charity. What would we do without you? The lot of us? Rot in the head, that's what. You get to a certain age, Samia, let me tell you, and there's a... the brain forgets, you know, forgets how to be a... You can

sit in a chair all day, like I sometimes do, and I'm spry for
my age, all things considered, but even I... you can sit in a
chair all day, and forget what it's like to be a person.

SAMIA. Oh Meg, don't say that.

MEG. But then there's you, coming in, popping by, cheerful, and
helpful, and hard-working despite it all, stirs the air up a bit.

SAMIA. It's nothing, really, Meg.

MEG. Oh these visits have become a lifeline, don't you know
it? Bet you hear that a lot.

SAMIA. I do.

MEG. Imagine having no one to talk to about Brussels sprouts.

SAMIA. I love that you do, by the way, nothing wrong with
sprouts.

MEG. I'm obsessed. Not Christmas without excessive talk of
Brussels sprouts. They call them Yorkshire sprouts now,
don't they? You'd go mad muttering 'sprouts' and 'chestnuts'
to yourself in that chair, start to doubt yourself.

Pause.

SAMIA. They giving you trouble? Your feet?

Pause.

MEG. It's been a long time, hasn't it, Samia?

SAMIA. What? That we've known each other? About a year,
give or take.

MEG. Since they locked us away like this, to die.

Pause.

SAMIA. It's quite the opposite, Meg, you know that.

Pause.

MEG. You start to doubt yourself. Has a day passed, has the
season? Have the bulbs taken, are there already daffodils?
The thing about sprouts, you see, is when they grow on the

stalk, remind me of a tree of bells, I used to think, if you shook them, they'd jingle, the sound of elves' feet, snow, and reindeer. I grew up where the snow crunched under your feet this time of year. Not that I'd know now, my feet have grown into the carpets.

Pause.

I look out the window, you know.

SAMIA. Yes, that's good.

MEG. I see the goings-on, I feel like a regular Havisham. Left at the altar.

SAMIA. Oh you're in a mood now, Meg, and it makes me sad.

MEG. I saw a young couple kissing on the street. I do get *lonely*, believe it or not, Samia, no, not in that papery old-person way, I get *horny*, Samia.

SAMIA. I'm sure you do, but –

MEG. Couldn't they sometimes send a handsome gentleman instead of you?

SAMIA. Are you asking me for sex?

MEG. No!

Pause.

SAMIA. Can we change the subject, Meg. I really want to stay here with you, I do, but can we keep things light? And social? And not talk about my job? Or these policies? I'm just... I'm really low down on the pecking order, you know that, Meg. I'm the smiling face. And I'm not even being cynical, you know what I mean? I'm happy to be here. I love you, in a way. Not in a way. I do, Meg, love you. Like my own nan.

MEG. She died...

SAMIA. She did die, got very sick and died, Meg, which is worth bringing up. Since you're going on about... I'm bound, professionally, to say, Meg, to *remind* you that my nan did get very sick, and died, and I don't like dwelling on it, obviously, because it's Christmas, but it's probably because it *is* Christmas, and the feelings are probably harder…

MEG. You're right, let's not dwell on it.

Silence.

SAMIA. Oh Meg. Come on. Could we put on some music?

MEG. Go on.

SAMIA *turns on the radio. A jaunty Christmas tune.*

SAMIA. Look, let's try to have a nice one, yeah? I'm here. You're here. We have each other. If briefly. There's sprouts. What'll you do with them?

MEG. Roast them, I reckon. Chestnuts. I don't do well with meat at my age. / Practically vegan nowadays.

SAMIA. Lush! And you've got your mulled wine, your naughty chocolates.

MEG. Drink makes me horny.

SAMIA. Would you like to dance a little? You like a good dance.

She tries to cajole MEG *into dancing.*

(*Singing.*) Come on, Meg. Meg! Get some exercise in. Come on.

MEG (*getting up*). Fine! Fine, fine.

They start dancing. Jaunty at first, then something comes over SAMIA. *She hugs* MEG *close, tightly.* SAMIA *gets emotional. They hug for several moments.*

MEG. You alright, Samia?

SAMIA (*turning off the radio*). I'm fine, I'm just so… I'm just aware of the time. And that I have to leave soon. And that you'll be here.

MEG. Oh Sam.

SAMIA. And I think of you unpacking your groceries. The food, the sprouts, roasting them, how happy that'll make you, how you'll sit here, in your chair, a big heaping tray of sprouts that you're never going to finish, and then what? Do you chuck them all in the fridge, or in the bin? And either way, they're going to yellow and sour and turn into shit. And I think, you've done nothing but talk about sprouts for a whole month now. And what'll it be like for you, seeing them turn to shit like that… after all that. And I think. This whole thing has us turned into shit from the inside out, hasn't it?

A long hug.

(*Recovering.*) Jesus. I should go, darling. It's getting dark.

MEG. Stay for dinner. Please. Help me with the sprouts.

A laugh.

SAMIA. I've got dinner, you know that.

MEG. Yes, Letty. And Hester. Alright.

SAMIA. Alright.

MEG. Merry Christmas.

Another hug.

(*Handing her a chocolate.*) One for the road. Yeah?

SAMIA (*taking one*). Alright. Bye then, love.

MEG. Bye. Do I see you…

SAMIA. After New Year's.

MEG. Right.

SAMIA *gathers her things, makes to go. Then –*

I want to leave, Samia.

SAMIA. What?

MEG. I want you to get me out of here.

Silence.

SAMIA. I can't do that. Don't even… Meg.

MEG. If you mean anything you've just said, if I'm to
believe… that you're a good person. Not like the one they
sent before you. Clinical. Medical. Pulling teeth to get a
word in. You care. You're not just government with a human
face, you care.

SAMIA. I do care, but.

MEG. I'm going mad.

SAMIA. Mad?

MEG. You saw earlier. With the calendar. I'm losing it, Samia.
The time. Time. I'm going to die of time.

SAMIA. You're not going to die. You're in rude health. You're
in perfect health. And –

MEG. I've got a big puffy coat.

SAMIA. What?

MEG. No one would even know.

SAMIA. Meg, stop.

MEG. One of those masks. Like yours. I've got one too. It'll be
fine. I've seen. From the window. You couldn't tell. I'm not
hunched. I don't shuffle.

SAMIA. For a walk, then, is that what you mean? A walk? Feel
the air a bit?

MEG. A walk. Yes. Something. To start?

SAMIA. To start?

Silence.

You don't mean.

MEG. I don't know.

SAMIA. You don't mean out of…

MEG. Out of the city? Yes. Tonight? Maybe? Soon? I don't know, I think I do. Out of the city. Out of... wherever it is, out of... God, Samia, out of prison, just take me out.

Silence.

SAMIA. If they caught us.

MEG. *If* they did, then.

SAMIA. I'd lose my job, worse... There's no way we wouldn't be caught.

MEG. You could do it. You're smart. I trust you.

Silence.

SAMIA. This isn't a prison, Meg. It's your home.

MEG. You know exactly what I mean.

SAMIA. I don't.

MEG. Why're you – why're you, why do you sound so –

Silence.

SAMIA. This is very inappropriate. It's very awkward. And unfair, on me.

MEG. Unfair?

SAMIA. There are proper... there are proper channels, Meg, is all I'm saying. I'm just the... you know, I've said, just the smiling face. If you have *problems* with the way... if you're having *issues* with your care... if you have *complaints*, there are numbers to call, offices, they can, I dunno, they could arrange for... maybe a change of flat, a different neighbourhood?

MEG. I don't want that.

SAMIA. Or a... could pair you up with a...

MEG. Don't want that either.

SAMIA. Maybe a cat. Not dogs. You like cats.

MEG. Unfair.

SAMIA. What?

MEG. Unfair, you said. Unfair on you.

SAMIA. It is. This is my job. You're… I *feel* like you're putting me in a very…

MEG. You get to go about. You get to get on with it. See people. Move. *Travel*, I assume. I look out the window. I can see. The goings-on. I've seen. The summer picnics. The all-night parties. Is it fancy dress?

SAMIA. What?

MEG. The Christmas party. The one you're going to?

SAMIA. There's no party.

MEG. You needn't lie to me. I can read your face. The guilt of it.

Pause.

You want to do more for me, don't you?

SAMIA. Do more?

Pause.

Need I remind you? You were the ones dropping off. It was your sad faces on the posters, on the ads, on the videos, on our minds all the fucking time.

MEG. You've never sworn at me before.

SAMIA. And you saw it all. Shut down. Again and again and again. And again. Imagine, Meg, three years of your life just taken away like that, three years of your prime life, Meg, three years I could've gotten rich, gotten ahead, gotten *on*, three years me and Letty could've found a place, gotten married, gotten *on*, two dogs died in three years, Meg, three years and I moved from my twenties to my thirties, Meg, three years is a generation, Meg, a whole *generation* stuck inside like fucking lepers. And now. Well, that was the consensus, you know that.

MEG....

SAMIA. *Do more*. Meg. We all agreed, didn't we? All waved goodbye, shut the doors, stopped the clocks, hoped for the best. Do more? By now we've surely done enough, above and beyond. Don't you think? Not like last time... You remember that... surely... I do. The chaos of it... the hideous... stupidity of... The ticker tape of doom. Magician's hands flapping about, misdirecting, making excuses, dropping the ball. But the ball's in our court now. I'm grateful, aren't you? That there's a future... least, we're all trying? Best outcomes. Best for all. Right? Optimised. On top of things. Firm grip, sure, bit hard in places, tight... tough love, expensive love, might I add. Sure. But it's a relief. A jab in the bum. And don't we need it, after all? After all that?

MEG....

SAMIA. Don't we feed and clean you, after all? When before, well... cold corpses on the divan, weren't it sometimes, often, the case?

MEG....

SAMIA. So. Yes, there's a party tonight. Parties. And I'm going. Letty and I are going. There'll be dancing, maybe, kissing, maybe, drinking and singing and crying, and there has been for months now, and there will be to come, because that was the consensus, that was the pact, that's what we all agreed to do.

MEG....

SAMIA. And it was done, you remember, out of love, and care, and sacrifice, a change to the national character. To move out the way, to give the young a shot, the booster engines falling off the rocket. And when you look out the window and see *life*, Meg, don't you feel it's... maybe, good? Good, after all, and fair, and *sad*, yes, obviously *sad*, but so is sickness, never-ending sickness, and death, that's also very sad?

MEG. You're crying.

SAMIA. Because I love you. And care. And maybe I shouldn't have showed you that. And treated you with kindness. I don't have to. It's not my job, you know? Cuz now you're here trying to abuse me, twist my arm, squeeze my heart, and, what? Meg, I have a life to live. You've put it at risk even bringing it up. Did you know that?

Pause.

Now, see, Meg, you really mustn't bring these things up. I'm bound, officially, Meg, to report these things.

MEG. What?

SAMIA. It's my job. You know. To report things.

MEG. You don't have to.

SAMIA. Well if it affects your care... somehow, or... if you're *unhappy*.

MEG. I am unhappy! Tell them that. I am unhappy. I am unhappy.

SAMIA. They'll have me transferred.

MEG. What?

SAMIA. They will. It's best practices.

MEG. No, I – that's not what I want, I'm saying *you* can take me, out, in secret, quietly, maybe, let me stay with...

SAMIA. Stay with?

MEG. Stay with you and Letty. And Hester.

Pause.

An alarm goes off from SAMIA*'s device. Shrill and beeping and urgent.*

SAMIA. Shit.

MEG. What's that?

SAMIA. I've stayed too long.

MEG. What?

SAMIA. Past the allotted time. They get funny when we stay too long.

MEG. Samia.

SAMIA. Sorry, Meg. I have to go.

MEG. Sorry, Samia.

SAMIA. It's probably best we don't see each other any more.

MEG. No, no.

SAMIA. They'll have me transferred, anyway. They will.

MEG. I won't bring it up again, we can... I'm sure they'll understand, too much to drink, too much sugar. The chocolate...

SAMIA. I brought the chocolate.

MEG. I'll say I had it snuck in. I –

SAMIA. It's not about the chocolate.

MEG. Samia, don't be angry.

SAMIA. I'm not angry, I'm –

MEG. You're so angry.

SAMIA. I'm disappointed.

MEG. Disappointed. I'm sorry.

SAMIA. Confused –

    MEG *starts to slap herself hard.*

    What are you –

MEG (*slapping*). I'm sorry.

SAMIA. Meg, stop.

MEG (*slapping herself continuously*). I don't know what I was thinking. I was so... overcome by... my body... wanted to... I think this is it, this is all there ever will be now... this smell... these... walls... this... I think I only have plastic knives. And there will never be red flowers again… or even daffodils, or men's smiles, and children, and love, or… Chocolate in crinkly foil. And I thought, I want to leave, I need to leave, this is not a life, this is not my life. And so… I opened myself to you, and, I'm sorry that it was not… appropriate, or fair, or even… I thought we had an understanding.

SAMIA. Please stop hitting yourself.

SAMIA *holds* MEG *until she calms down, gradually. Over this:*

MEG. I forgot, for a moment, forgot myself. Forgot. Forgot this is good, after all, and right, and, better than death, and life continues, and life goes on, and this is good, after all, for you, especially you, and Letty and Hester, and all of you, the kissing, and the dancing, and the smiles… maybe next time you could just bring me some daffodils?

SAMIA. I don't know, Meg.

Pause.

MEG. Don't make a report.

SAMIA. They've probably already…

MEG. What?

SAMIA. They record, you know.

MEG. What?

SAMIA. You know this. They record our visits.

MEG. They.

SAMIA. For training purposes. For safety, not that there's anything to be *safe* from, but you never know, especially with the men…

MEG. They've recorded?

SAMIA. I don't know if they're *listening* but.

MEG. But.

SAMIA. The alarm's gone off, so they might.

MEG. Might.

SAMIA. Might check to see, and...

MEG. No, no...

SAMIA. Well, listen, we could... on record. To be official, if you... I could... I'll ask you some questions, a survey, you know, about your care? And all you'd have to do is answer the right way, do you understand, Meg?

MEG. Yes.

SAMIA. Do you really, Meg? Be clever here. Do you?

MEG. Yes. I do.

SAMIA *holds up a camera to record* MEG.

SAMIA. Good. So. Smile. That's it. Okay. Meg, are you satisfied with the quality of my care?

MEG. Yes.

SAMIA. Meg, are you satisfied with the conditions of your care?

MEG. Yes.

SAMIA. Are you satisfied with the conditions of your home?

MEG. Yes.

SAMIA. Do you have any issues you would like to raise with the conditions of your care or the performance of your carer?

MEG. No.

SAMIA. Thank you, Meg. Your thumbprint.

MEG *prints her thumb on the device.*

MEG. Will that...

SAMIA. I should think so. I should hope so.

MEG. Okay. Will you...

SAMIA. I'm on your side, Meg.

MEG. Yes. Thank you.

SAMIA. I'm sorry about… but it's not forever, is it?

MEG. No, not forever.

SAMIA. And meanwhile, it's… thank you. I know it's hard.

MEG. It is.

SAMIA. But you're strong, Meg.

MEG. I am.

SAMIA. I do love you.

MEG. I love you too.

They hug.

This world is nothing without being young, is it? Nothing without the noise and music. The sex and parties.

SAMIA. Nothing at all.

MEG. And this is who we are, after all.

SAMIA. And what's that?

MEG. People who look after each other.

SAMIA. Yes.

MEG. And who are looked after.

SAMIA. Yes. We look after each other.

Silence. It's now fully dark outside. The two women stare hard at each other.

Have you had a good Christmas, then, Meg?

MEG. I'm tired.

SAMIA. You're tired.

MEG. Very tired.

SAMIA. It's the sugar rush, it's coming down. The adrenalin. Do you want to take a rest? A little post-Christmas nap?

MEG. Yes please.

SAMIA. Here on the chair, then. That alright?

MEG. Yes.

SAMIA. I'm sorry we had a row.

MEG. Me too. It was my fault.

SAMIA *puts* MEG *back into the chair. Tucks a blanket round her.*

SAMIA. Do you need help cleaning up?

MEG. I can do it later, don't want to keep you.

SAMIA. Yeah? Alright then. Thank you, Meg.

MEG. Thank you, Samia.

SAMIA. Merry Christmas.

MEG. Merry Christmas.

SAMIA. And Happy New Year's.

MEG. And that.

SAMIA *gets up, puts on her things. Her overcoat. Her mask. She turns to see that* MEG *is dozing off.* SAMIA *makes to leave.*

Samia.

SAMIA. Yes, love?

MEG. The calendar.

SAMIA. Yes, Meg, what about?

MEG. The date on that is wrong, isn't it? I'm not imagining it.

SAMIA. You are, Meg.

MEG. I really could have sworn.

SAMIA. What was that, Meg?

MEG. That it was the wrong year. And I thought to myself,
holding it, the calendar, is it the wrong year? Is it after all?
And honestly, there are days I think it's best not to know.
There is sometimes snow in April, isn't there? And isn't it
always grey, anyway, and anyway the days are grey in your
old age, Samia...

SAMIA. Merry Christmas, Meg.

MEG. They don't say foggy for nothing...

SAMIA *fixes her face and quietly exits over this speech.*
MEG, *alone again in her chair.*

Samia, inside the walls are the same walls as any other day.
Samia, inside, you know, the weeks are new bedding, and the
trash building up, the time it takes for apples to go soft in the
fridge, and so I wondered, and maybe this is something to
raise, I've been thinking of the time, and the days, or the
date, and a *calendar* with the wrong year, and I've
wondered, is it... is it even Christmas after all? And does it
matter, after all?

The End.

Ursa Major

Joe White

For Nell

Characters

JAY, *young, male*
CALLISTO, *old, female*

A forward slash (/) marks the point at which the next speaker interrupts.

One

Self-service checkout of a supermarket. Late.

JAY is on the phone. He's a little tipsy. He wears a mask and gloves. Outside the weather is treacherous.

JAY. Hi, uh, so, I know you said not to call… And. Like. Specially –

Beep.

Specially not like midnight on a Tuesday, but, I'm not – this isn't some – some – some *excuse* to call you, this isn't for *me*, is what I'm saying, this is actually important, okay –

Beep.

You left your Laura Ashley lamp. And, uh – So I was thinking, maybe – You needed to come get that. Some time.

Beep.

And maybe, when you did, we could. You know. Talk –

Please place the item in the / bagging area.

/ Sorry, hang on, I'm just in the, uh –

Unexpected item in the bagging area / please remove item –

/ Oh for f… sorry…

Item removed from the bagging area.

Just me, or was it always this hard / to do your –

/ *Please place the item / in the bagging area –*

/ Anyway, what I'm saying / is that –

/ *Unexpected item in / the bagging area –*

/ How is it unexpected? / She just said put it in the –
bagging –

/ Please remove item from the bagging area.

There.

Item removed from bagging area.

What I'm trying to say is that I really love you –

Please place / item in the bagging area –

/ YOU KNOW WHAT – HOW'S THIS FOR PLACING IT
IN THE BAGGING AREA? YOU FEEL THAT? YOU
FEEL ANYTHING YOU HEARTLESS BI–

Two

The road outside. Wet and freezing. We hear the rain.

JAY *is sat there, lost.*

CALLI *is stood.*

CALLI. Everything okay?

JAY. Huh?

CALLI. You want me to grab you something to eat?

   Beat.

JAY. I'm not… I'm not homeless.

CALLI. Okay –

JAY. They kicked me out. I had a thing with the self-service till.

CALLI. Good for you. About time someone fought back – the
   bastards.

JAY. Yeah.

CALLI. First sign of the revolution right there.

JAY. Right?

What?

CALLI. The singularity? Oh yeah, it's been and gone. These things are sentient now, they're choosing to fuck with us, it's terrorism really.

JAY. Right.

Well nice meeting you anyway –

CALLI. I've seen you.

JAY. What?

CALLI. You've got a dog, right? Little white thing – looks like a slipper.

JAY *nods*.

I've seen you and your girlfriend dragging that thing around the / park.

JAY. / Wife.

CALLI. What?

JAY. My wife.

CALLI. What religion?

JAY. What?

CALLI. You're young.

JAY. Yeah, no, we've been together since we were ten. Not. Religious.

CALLI. Oh. Well. Good for you.

JAY. Always been together, you know. One of those annoying couples. Real love…

A long pause. She just looks at him, and he's held by it.

You live near the park?

CALLI. Sure. 'Near'. 'In'. Whatever.

JAY. Sorry?

CALLI. Problem is, the park's so open, you know – in winter the wind cuts right through. And in summer you get all the junkies flooding in. But in spring, sure I stay in the park.

Beat.

JAY. So. You're. Homeless?

CALLI. I'm *houseless*. I have a tent.

JAY. Right… but you're…

CALLI. What?

JAY. Quite… M-m-mature.

CALLI. Well, that's a word.

JAY. Sorry –

CALLI. People tend to use mature for cheese and porn stars.

JAY. I wouldn't know.

CALLI. What, you don't eat cheese?

JAY. Not that kind of cheese –

CALLI. I'm not some wild woman, okay, I haven't been living in a cave all my life. I've lived in flats and houses. All over the world in fact. In Japan and Egypt and Uzbekistan and Kenya. I've lived in an Iroquois longhouse, a Mongolian ger and a Renaissance chateau with the Duke of Magenta. For ten months I stayed in the kitchen of a Pizza Hut with a guitarist called Chip. I've slept under slate, and skin, and dung, and stars, and none of those places – not one – has ever defined who I am, or where I'm from, or how you get to see me, okay, I was just asking if you needed help.

She goes.

JAY. Uh, wait a second, wait, wait – I'm sorry – I'm a bit drunk and, uh, I've had a bit of a… Let me – let me pay for your – For / whatever you were going in there for –

CALLI. / You don't have to do that – it's fine –

JAY. No, I-I do, I want to. I'm a good person. I am. I give ten pounds a month to the donkey sanctuary.

CALLI. Well, when you put it like that –

JAY. And maybe you could. Buy some food for me too. / They took mine off me.

CALLI. / Ha. Sure.

JAY. Here's my, uh. List. And here's, uh. Ten pounds. Twenty. Spend-Spend it all –

CALLI. Can I get a microwave meal?

JAY. Sure, whatever you want.

CALLI. And then can I borrow your microwave?

Beat.

You have a microwave, right?

JAY. Yeah, but –

CALLI. I haven't had a hot meal in three weeks. I'd really like to eat something hot tonight.

Pause.

JAY. Okay, look, uh, okay, how about this. Uh. How about we go back to mine, I-I take the meal up to my flat. Microwave it. And bring it back out to you…? With a fork.

CALLI. What do you think is gonna happen in your flat? You think I'm gonna have my way with you? / Cos you're not my type.

JAY. / No, I don't think – okay, well likewise – no, it's just I'm a bit, I'm quite, uh, particular, about – My-my wife says I'm OCD with things. Hygiene things. Since, you know – She says I'm insane, actually, that it drives her absolutely insane –

CALLI. Can you see me?

Hello?

JAY. Hello –

CALLI. I'm actually here, man, I'm stood in front of you, right now, I'm a real person, stood here in front of you – looking you in the eye and asking for a hot meal and a place to eat it. Ten minutes, that's it. I mean, isn't that something a good person would do? Isn't that better than a donkey sanctuary? Or will your wife have a problem with me coming in?

…

I'll go get your shopping.

Three

Their flat.

JAY *still wears his mask and gloves.*

JAY. So, yeah, uh. This is the living room. Sorry, I just need to, test this uh…

He flicks the light on and off six times.

The light switch is a bit… Okay, that's fixed, uh – You can – Uh – You can sit-sit on that chair, there, uh. There's some. Uh. Sanitiser, there. If you wouldn't – I'm careful.

CALLI. That's one word for it.

JAY. Yeah, yes. So. As you can see, everything in here's pretty, uh, pretty –

CALLI. Beige.

JAY. Ha. Yeah. And *clean*. So –

CALLI. All that's missing is one of those 'Live Laugh Love' signs.

JAY. Yeah. Yeah… The mantelpiece –

CALLI. Oh. There it is.

JAY. My wife's. Yeah.

CALLI. She got a name?

JAY. Tobi. With an 'I', yeah, she's not here.

CALLI. I noticed.

JAY. She's seeing her mum. With the dog. For, like, a week or so... I'll put this in the microwave...

He thinks about whether he should leave her, then goes.

CALLI (*calling*). So... How much does a fine chunk of beige cost these days?

JAY (*off*). Uh. Nine hundred a month.

CALLI (*calling*). Pounds?

JAY (*off*). Each.

CALLI (*calling*). *Each?*

JAY (*off*). We were lucky. After the pandemic the rents really fell. It was nine-two-five before... (*Entering.*) That will be just be a minute – Oh, hang on – Bloody light again – You notice it flickering?

CALLI. No –

JAY. Hang on...

He does it again. Six times.

CALLI. You have to do that every time you come in the room, huh.

JAY. What?

CALLI. Hit the switch on and off six times.

JAY. No, was that – Was that six –

CALLI. And can you take your mask off please, for God's sake, I'm sat in your flat and I don't even know what you look like.

He pulls down his mask a tiny bit. Then a bit more.

JAY (*whilst pulling his mask*). I-I don't count / the light –

CALLI. / See. Much better. Nice face.

JAY.…Is it?

CALLI. Yes. Very handsome. Kind.

> JAY *removes his mask entirely, but keeps his gloves on.*

> Look, I know it's been a while, but seeing as I'm here, why don't you at least pretend this is a normal interaction. I don't even know your name –

JAY. It's Jay. I'm Jay –

CALLI. Nice to meet you, Jay. I'm Calli. Callisto.

JAY. Ca… Callisto?

CALLI. Like the nymph.

JAY. And the moon.

CALLI. What?

JAY. Callisto is the name of Jupiter's second largest moon.

CALLI. Only second largest, huh –

JAY. And, also, uh, a constellation is named after you. Well, not you. The original Callisto.

CALLI. The nymph.

JAY. Ursa Major. The Great Bear… I'm a – I'm a Research Fellow at UCL. Observational Cosmology. So. Yeah. Your name's pretty big in my world.

CALLI. My world too.

> JAY *smiles.*

> *The microwave pings.*

JAY. Uh – That – That will be your dinner… Your ten minutes starts now. Ha…

He goes to get it. CALLI *starts looking around the flat –
touching things.*

CALLI (*calling*). So, you study stars.

JAY (*off*). Well, more like everything in between, really… Dark
energy…

CALLI (*calling*). What?

JAY (*off*). W-well, uh, in a-in a nutshell, you've got matter…
okay… which is everything we know, you know, like, atoms,
galaxies, the moon, me, you – ow fuck, that's hot – But, but,
uh, matter only makes up about five per cent of the known
universe. So what's the rest?

CALLI (*sotto voce*). I dunno, estate agents?

JAY (*off*). We think twenty-seven per cent of it is this thing
called dark matter, okay. And sixty-eight per cent of it is this
thing called dark *energy*, both of which are invisible, but we
know the effects of dark energy, we can see that it is pushing
things further and further apart… all the time… (*Entering
with the meal.*) I mean every second, every millisecond,
everything that exists in the entire universe is…

He places the meal on the floor and backs away.

Distancing…

CALLI *stares at the food on the floor for a few moments.*

What?

CALLI. I'm just wondering what trick I should I do? You want
me to play dead maybe, roll over, you can scratch my belly –

JAY. What?

CALLI. Pick that up – What the hell do / you think I am,
putting it on the floor –

JAY. / Sorry. I was just – Sorry…

He picks it up and hands it to her, from a distance.

CALLI. And I don't get a plate? A nice beige plate?

JAY. Uh –

CALLI. It's fine, it'll do, Jesus, you can't teach class.

> JAY *looks at the light.*

> You not eating?

JAY. No. Uh, no. Not yet –

CALLI. Well then can you sit down, at least? You'll give me indigestion.

JAY. Uh, yeah –

CALLI. And don't even think about touching that fucking light switch again, okay –

JAY. Okay.

> *He sits a distance away. As she eats and talks, we hear the weather outside get worse.*

CALLI. So.

> You were saying…

JAY. What?

CALLI (*mouth full*). You study the mysterious distancing of the universe –

JAY. Well –

CALLI. Trying to work out why gaps grow between things.

JAY. Well, stars mainly –

CALLI. But not people.

JAY. What?

CALLI. Well, it's all matter, right? I mean if it's out there, it's down here too. Must work on us as well… It's your turn now.

JAY. What?

CALLI. To ask me something about my life.

JAY. Like what?

CALLI. Like, I dunno, like just make some fucking conversation with / me like a normal fucking –

JAY. / Sorry, okay, alright – How – How long have you been homeless?

CALLI. Oh Jesus –

JAY. Houseless / sorry –

CALLI. / Always this – I've never owned a house, have you?

JAY. No.

CALLI. Well then you see how fucking boring that question is.

JAY. Yeah but I'm not the one sleeping in a tent.

CALLI. You think someone's forcing me to do that? I'm a little old lady, Jay, I'm a British citizen. Even those human gall bladders in Westminster couldn't force me to do that –

JAY. So it's your choice then?

CALLI. Yes.

JAY. Why?

CALLI. Because I have one. Because I'm lucky enough to / have one –

JAY. / Lucky.

CALLI. Lucky to be educated, yes. Lucky to be born where I was, *when* I was; outside of war or genocide or climate migration; lucky to speak English; lucky to be white –

JAY. Lucky to / be white –

CALLI. / Lucky to opt out of a society where this 'luck' counts. You understand?

The only type of person living on the streets should be like me, but they're not, cos they don't have the luck I have and that's fucking terrible, do you understand?

JAY. Yes.

CALLI. Good now ask me another question, and no more
politics please, I'm trying to eat.

Beat.

JAY. Uh... Have-Have you ever been married?

CALLI. Oh God – out of the frying pan –

JAY. I-I can ask something else –

CALLI. No. You asked.

I met a guy called Trevor while I was studying in Italy. I
was eighteen. My roommate was in love with him, but...
Anyway, I ended up in London, and then he ended up in
London and we got together and lived together. I was a
very young, very naive... *girl*. And I got pregnant. We tried
to get an abortion – it had just become legal then – but they
turned me down. So we got married. Such a charming
polite young man. Good looking. Soft spoken. Sweet,
really. A painter. He painted portraits. I worked. Washed
dishes. Cleaned houses. Then I got a job at Glyndebourne,
you know, the opera company? We moved to Sussex. I was
working all hours of the day and night and he was all alone
and couldn't cope with the baby. And he beat her up. Me
too. Repeatedly, over a period of time. Finally, I took the
baby and ran away to a friend's. And the police arrested
him on opening night of the Glyndebourne season, and
when it made the newspapers I lost my job. They took the
baby into care, put her in hospital, Trevor in prison. He hit
his head against the bars, so they moved him to a
psychiatric ward. And then I got hit by a car. While I was
cycling home one night. Broke some bones, legs, arms,
stuff like that. So I was in hospital too. Six months. And
when I came out I decided the best thing I could do was put
her up for adoption. Which was...

The sound of the rain. She thinks for a moment.

But her foster parents wanted her – they said 'if you don't let
us have her, we'll take you to court', so I thought 'they must
really want her'. And, I, uh, I couldn't get a divorce from

Trevor because we hadn't been married for two years and I couldn't get it on special grounds – I mean if that's not special grounds, I don't know what is... Anyway. Time passed. Years. I had boyfriends. Children as well. I lived all over. At some point, I got a notification that the divorce was through... And then, a million years later, I was teaching, somewhere, and I got a call from an ex, who'd had a call from an ex saying that Trevor had been eaten by a bear whilst hiking in Jesper National Park... And I was horrified, because they shot the bear. I mean it was only doing its karmic duty, you know?

So. Yes. I've been married.

Beat.

I bet you haven't thought about the light switch once.

Beat.

JAY. Did... Did you ever... See her again? The baby?

CALLI. Well. I'd developed some medical things over the years. Genetic. Hereditary stuff. And I thought she should know. So I messaged her and said I'm really sorry to do this on Facebook, but I'm your birth mother, and would you like to meet? And she sent back a message saying 'Yeah okay'. Like that. 'Yeah okay, and I'll meet you on such-and-such a day. In Brighton.' And. So we met. And... It was like seeing myself. When she walked towards me... it was like looking at a mirror, of *history*. She looked just like me. But twenty years younger. The first thing she said to me was 'you did the right thing... I had wonderful parents and a wonderful life'. I said, that's all I wanted to know. She was quite angry. Yes, quite angry, but we spent a few hours together all the same. Talking. Standing. About the distance you are now. All that distance between us. I so wanted to hug her. Just once. But. She didn't. So that was that...

Beat.

JAY. ....And that's – That was it? You – you didn't contact her again –

CALLI. No, I did. I messaged but she blocked me, and I had to respect that...

JAY. But... I mean, but –

CALLI. Just cos you love something, doesn't mean you get to control it, you know. Or even understand it. That's futile. It's like. Thinking that flicking a light switch might bring someone back...

She smiles at JAY, *sadly. He doesn't know what to say.*

A while. The rain.

You wanna talk about / it –

JAY. / No.

CALLI. Why not?

He scoffs, hangs his head – can't look at her.

Cos I'm a stranger? Or. Cos then it's real? Once it's out loud. Then it's... like matter...

He looks at her, sort of impressed with the analogy.

My ex-husband got eaten by a bear, okay, I've heard it all.

He smiles, sighs, takes his time.

JAY. ....I'd done her a bath. With a bath bomb, you know what that is? Drop it in the bath –

CALLI. I know what a bath bomb is –

JAY. Right, well this was a *galaxy* one. One that was s'posed to look like a galaxy. Basically dyed the water dark blue, lots of glitter, swirling. It didn't look like any galaxy I know. Before that, she'd said I didn't do things for her – like spontaneous things, romantic, uh... *Intimate*... So, I did this bath, but she said she was tired from work, and I should get in if I wanted. And course I didn't, but the bath bomb cost a fiver, so I did, and she must have felt bad, or something, cos she started washing my hair. In the bath. Which was really – I can't remember the last time someone washed my hair... This is probably too much information, but we hadn't been intimate in, in, in, like a few months, so her touching my hair was – It had a physiological effect. Uh. And, I'm sat there with… that, like, sticking out of the cosmos, my body covered in glitter, hair all foamy, and I ask her if she thought we'd grown apart and she said she did and I asked if she knew why and she said because she didn't love me any more… Uh. And then she – Then she left the room. And. It was… Like I couldn't hear…? And I don't know how long I was there, but then I realised there weren't any towels. So I had to go to the bedroom, all… And she was – she looked at me, and her face, sort of curled up, and she said 'we're not having sex if that's what you think' and I said of course that's not what I think, you just broke my heart. And then I. Begged her. I got on my knees, and begged her to love me again… But she said it had gone and she didn't know how to get it back and that was that.

Last person I…

Even in the shops I don't…

Do you think she's gonna come back?

You can say it, I can take it…

Maybe I need to hear it. Maybe that's what I need.

Beat.

CALLI. Well –

JAY. Okay, actually I don't need that –

CALLI. Okay.

JAY. I know. I know…

I've got enough rent for another month. Basically. Then…

He shrugs.

CALLI. You'll be houseless too…

JAY *nods. He's holding it together.*

Oh, I so wanna hug you right now…

JAY. Ha. Uh…

The moment passes.

(*Re: the food.*) You all done?

CALLI. Yeah. Uh. Shall I put it down on the [floor]?

JAY. No, no, I'll take it… Uh…

JAY *moves to her, then removes his gloves and takes the plate. She smiles, takes his hand. Holds it. Stares at him. He wants to pull his hand away, but doesn't. He looks at her. A few moments.*

CALLI. You'll be okay, you know.

Take it from me. You will.

JAY *cries.*

He holds her. She holds him back. They hold as long as they need to.

I guess that's my ten minutes…

JAY. Yeah… uh…

CALLI *gets her things.*

Unless, you know… The weather's really bad and – If it's – If it's not weird or anything – You know and just say if you think it's weird – But I could, I mean, I could do the sofa up for you…? I-I've got blankets and… You could stay… Couple of nights, I dunno, a week…

CALLI *smiles at him.*

CALLI. Don't touch that switch again after you've turned it off, okay?

That's all you have to do tonight.

You're gonna be okay.

JAY *smiles as* CALLI *leaves.*

JAY *looks at his wedding ring. He lets out a sigh. He turns the light off. He doesn't turn it back on again.*

The End.

Outside

Outside was first performed and livestreamed from the Orange Tree Theatre, Richmond, on 15 April 2021. The cast and creative team were as follows:

Two Billion Beats   by Sonali Bhattacharyya
Cast not confirmed at time of publication

The Kiss   by Zoe Cooper
LOU   Temi Wilkey

Prodigal   by Kalungi Ssebandeke
Cast not confirmed at time of publication

Director	Georgia Green
Designer	Camilla Clarke
Lighting Designer	Rajiv Pattani
Sound Designer & Composer	Mwen Rukandema
Casting	Sarah Murray
Company Stage Manager	Jenny Skivens
Stage Manager	Caoimhe Regan

The *Inside/Outside* series of plays was curated by Guy Jones, Orange Tree Literary Associate

Two Billion Beats

Sonali Bhattacharyya

Characters

ASHA, *seventeen, British Asian rude girl, mouth and trousers*
BETTINA, *fifteen, a quiet daydreamer prone to flights of fancy*

ASHA *is cleaning graffiti off the gates at the front of her sixth-form college, in her school uniform, headphones in.*

BETTINA, *also in school uniform, watches* ASHA *work.*

ASHA *pauses to recount the events leading up to this to the audience.*

ASHA (*direct address*). You start with something surprising, something clickbaity. 'You won't believe what she looks like now!' That sort of thing, you know? Mrs L loves that shit. She calls it 'opening with a flourish'. *Gandhi didn't use his fists, but he was still a fighter. How did this skinny man in glasses take on the might of the British empire, and win?* Then I go in with a killer quote, show I've done my research. *'In a gentle way, you can shake the world.'* And then *'Whenever you are confronted with an opponent, conquer him with love.' These quotes, which made up what we now understand to be Gandhi's philosophy, have withstood the test of time because of the ongoing importance the struggle against injustice has for us still, in modern times. How can ordinary people make a difference against forces much more powerful than us?* Yeah, I know right? *But when considering 'Can the pen be mightier than the sword?'* – keep bringing it back to the essay question, like the examiners have got Alzheimer's or something, that's what Mrs L says. Not exactly that, but basically, yeah. *When considering 'Can the pen be mightier than the sword?' it's important to remember that Gandhi didn't just write about his ideas, he saw them through in his own life. When he wrote about fasting as a tool of resistance, he didn't just expect other people to do it. He fasted too – eighteen times. The longest he fastest for was twenty-one days. For Gandhi, fasting was a 'weapon', even if it was a non-violent one. He didn't always use it against the British, though. Sometimes he used this weapon against his fellow Indians.* Boom, that's the hook. Controversh. If you haven't got their attention now, you might

as well pack it in. *When Gandhi and another giant in the
Indian struggle for independence didn't see eye to eye on the
rights of untouchables, or 'dalits', in the new government,
Gandhi started to fast. Ambedkar, the dalit leader who was
chair of the committee who drafted India's constitution, called
the fast a 'stunt', but Gandhi was too stubborn to back down.
Ambedkar wanted dalits to have their own elections, free from
interference or intimidation by high-caste Hindus. He said 'I
want political power for my community. That is indispensible
for our survival.'* Another quote, yeah? Mrs L loved that one.
Said it spoke to her from history. *Gandhi was worried
Ambedkar's proposal would divide Hindus and lead to
bloodshed. He believed high-caste Hindus must be
encouraged to have a change of heart. Ambedkar believed
dalits' rights couldn't wait, but eventually backed down, as the
press sided with Gandhi. He didn't want his community to be
blamed for Gandhi's death. So the pen can be mightier than
the sword, but it isn't always clear if the right person wins.*

BETTINA. So what did you get on your essay then?

ASHA *returns to cleaning the graffiti from the gates.*

ASHA. Eighty per cent. Correct and appropriate use of archival
materials – tick. Good understanding of the interpretations
put forward in the extract – tick. Strong awareness of
historical context – tick. Well supported and convincing
evaluation of the arguments – tick, tick, tick. Mrs L said,
between me and her, it was the best mock exam paper she'd
seen in all her years. Straight up, thought she was going to
cry.

BETTINA. Lolz. Knocked it out Sunday evening between
Assassin's Creed sessions, didn't you?

ASHA. Haha. Yeah… (*Direct address.*) *No*. Spent two weeks
doing research and pulled three all-nighters writing three,
no… *four* drafts… Mrs L said I should draw on my personal
experience more often, and she only started to really enjoy
history after she discovered Emmeline Pankhurst, which was
just… *weird*. And I didn't know what to say, so I didn't say

anything. And anyway, it was break time and I had two free periods. (*To* BETTINA.) Thought I'd be picking up Mickey Ds on my way home by now.

BETTINA. So how come you're out here?

ASHA. Because Mrs L's a fucking bitch.

BETTINA (*re: the cleaner*). You're using the wrong one, you know? It'll come off easier if you use that one.

ASHA. What?

BETTINA. You want the kind that smells a bit like cooking oil? And... a brush with hard bristles. Like this one.

ASHA. Did I ask for your advice?

BETTINA. You need an oil-based cleaner for an oil-based paint.

ASHA. Did I ask for your *help*?

BETTINA. Otherwise you're creating an emulsion.

ASHA. What do you know about emulsions?

BETTINA. I'm only trying to help.

ASHA. Let me get on with it then.

BETTINA. Sorry for breathing.

ASHA. It's coming off.

BETTINA. *Bare* slow, though. Bus'll be here in fifteen minutes.

ASHA. Don't miss it.

BETTINA *sits down, takes out a bag of crisps from her bag. Offers* ASHA *one.*

ASHA. No thanks.

BETTINA. What's it say?

ASHA. Know how to read, don't you?

BETTINA. Yeah. But why does it say that? 'Live'?

ASHA. How should I know?

BETTINA. Why'd you paint it?

ASHA. Who's to say I did?

BETTINA....Then why're you cleaning it?

ASHA. Because I'm a good Samaritan.

BETTINA. What?

ASHA. Because I'm a community champion.

BETTINA. Mrs L put you on detention?

ASHA. What do you think?

BETTINA. She's always seemed alright to me.

ASHA. Used to think so too.

BETTINA. She seems friendly in the playground.

ASHA. Not the same as being in her class. She's different with the little kids.

BETTINA. I'm not a little kid.

ASHA. Year 10 is little.

BETTINA. Heard about the common room. With Mel Summers.

ASHA. You can't go by the timetable for that stop. Bus could come any minute.

BETTINA. I'll get the next one. You'll be done by then.

ASHA. I'm not sitting with you.

BETTINA. Why not?

ASHA. I'm walking. Going round Rommi's on the way home. Go wait at the stop.

BETTINA. No.

ASHA. *Bettina.*

BETTINA. I won't.

> ASHA *tries to push her towards the bus stop.* BETTINA *doesn't budge, showing impressive passive resistance. Hurt beat.* BETTINA *straightens her jacket, etc.*

ASHA. What do you want to hang around here for?

BETTINA. Steph and Milo and that lot get that bus.

ASHA. So...?

BETTINA. ...You'll be cross.

ASHA. What have they been doing?

BETTINA. They make me pay an extra fare. To go upstairs.

ASHA. An upstairs fare?

BETTINA. Mm-hmm.

ASHA. So you've told them to fuck off, right?

BETTINA. No.

ASHA. Why not?

BETTINA. It's easy for you to say.

ASHA. It's easy for everyone to say. Fuck and off. There. Try it.

BETTINA. I just started sitting downstairs. Near the front, where the driver is. And that worked for a bit. But now they're started charging me a door fare.

ASHA. A door fare?

BETTINA. Yeah.

ASHA. As in, when you want to get off?

BETTINA. Yeah.

ASHA. And this time you definitely told them to fuck off, right?

BETTINA. Been using my birthday money but it's run out now.

ASHA. You serious?

BETTINA. Don't tell Mum.

ASHA. She pays for your travel card up front.

BETTINA. I know.

ASHA. So she's paying *double*?

BETTINA. I know.

ASHA. Because of Steph, Lee and Milo...?

BETTINA. You're not going to tell, are you? Told her I was saving up.

ASHA. Didn't think that one through then, did you?

BETTINA. That's what I would have been doing.

ASHA. Saving for what?

BETTINA. I want a hamster.

    Beat.

ASHA. No.

BETTINA. You can't stop me.

ASHA. I don't have to. Steph and Lee and Milo are seeing to that, aren't they?

BETTINA. I'll keep it on my side of the room.

ASHA. Got to be kidding. It'll stink the place out.

BETTINA. They're really clean.

ASHA. They're vermin.

BETTINA. That's not true. Look. It's this one, in the pet shop in the mall...

    BETTINA *finds a photo on her phone.*

ASHA. Why have you got a picture of it?

BETTINA. It's so cute. Look at its little nose.

ASHA. Let me see.

She looks at BETTINA*'s phone again.*

That's not a hamster.

BETTINA. It is.

ASHA. It's not. It's too big to be a hamster. It's like... I dunno... That's a guinea pig or something.

BETTINA. He wants thirty-four ninety-nine for the cage and the sawdust and the food and I almost had enough, yeah? But now I've got, like, two pounds fifty. And that's only if I don't get the bus today.

ASHA. Need to learn to stand up for yourself.

BETTINA. If I tell them to fuck off I'll just get slaps.

ASHA. How do you know if you don't even try?

BETTINA. I'm not like you.

ASHA. You don't have to be like me.

BETTINA. Yeah, alright. But how do I be like me and keep my birthday money?

ASHA. ...Maybe you should get a bike.

BETTINA. I'm rubbish on a bike.

ASHA. You'll get the hang of it.

BETTINA. They wouldn't dare pick on me if they knew you were my sister.

Especially after what happened this afternoon.

ASHA. You don't know what you're talking about.

BETTINA. I heard you marched into the common room, eyes blazing, torpedoed in on Mel Summers and slapped her until her head was spinning.

ASHA. No.

BETTINA. Heard she didn't stand a chance. That it took three people to pull you off her.

ASHA. That's not what happened.

BETTINA. Heard you were like *fire*. Righteous *fire*.

ASHA. I didn't go into the common room looking for Mel, or
looking for trouble, or looking for *anyone*. I was hungry. I
just wanted some Quavers.

BETTINA *offers up her crisps again, but* ASHA *doesn't
notice.*

(*Direct address.*) I was thinking about what Mrs L had said.
'Draw on your personal experience.' Couldn't get that out of
my head. What did she mean? Gandhiji? Or Ambedkar? Or
did she mean both? Cos there is a massive difference, yeah?
Like, Ambedkar's trying his best to do everything right. Tick
all the boxes. Gandhi pulls a tantrum and whatever
Ambedkar does, he ends up as the bad guy... Plus they're a
couple of dudes. *Old* dudes. *Dead* dudes. And why wouldn't
Emmeline Pankhurst be my experience? Is that what she
meant? I mean, she's dead too...

BETTINA. ...*You* could tell them to fuck off?

ASHA. What?

BETTINA. Milo and Steph and that lot?

ASHA. You need me to do that for you?

BETTINA. And maybe you could, like, push them around a bit?
Blake – he's the biggest. No, Steph. She's the scariest. Yeah,
Steph.

ASHA. You want me to get on the bus and beat up Steph? In
front of everyone?

BETTINA. Yeah. Or, it doesn't have to be on the bus. It could
be out here. Or... or... in the common room again? That
would be good. That would really send a *message*.

ASHA. And then what?

BETTINA. ...They leave me alone and I can start saving up
again.

ASHA. And then what for me?

Beat. BETTINA *looks at all the cleaning products, and the graffiti.*

BETTINA. Just get on the bus with me, then. They don't have to know I'm your sister. Especially after what happened in the common room.

ASHA. You don't even know what happened in the common room.

BETTINA. They just have to think you like me.

ASHA. I do like you.

BETTINA. So why won't you do it, then?

ASHA. You know this is the first time I've ever been in detention? And, like, I've been close time and time again. Lost count of how many orange cards I've been on. But I always pull it back, right from the brink.

BETTINA. Course. As if they'd dare put the smartest kid in college on suspension.

ASHA. I'm not the smartest kid in college.

BETTINA. Who's smarter?

ASHA. But now I've got a suspension on my school record, eight months before I'm going to send out my UCAS. And I'm not risking getting another one just so you can buy a guinea pig.

BETTINA. It's a hamster.

ASHA. That is not a hamster, Bettina. It's too big to be a hamster.

BETTINA. I know it's a hamster, because I had a dream about it. I had a dream it was running and running, you know, on the little wheel they have? And it was scared, because it knew something was following it. Not actually following it, in the pet shop. But somewhere, out there, something was after it, and even though it didn't make any sense, it had to run, it just had to. Because that was the only way to get rid of the panic it could feel setting in. And when I woke up my heart was *pounding* and I was out of breath.

ASHA. You think you're a hamster?

BETTINA. No... I just mean... It's scared, and I want to bring it home and look after it.

ASHA. Maybe it's you it's scared of. Gawking at it through the window, taking photos.

BETTINA. No...

ASHA. 'Doesn't she have anything better to do?' Doesn't she have, like, fucking homework?

BETTINA. No one is scared of me. That is the problem. Their hearts beat fast because they're so little, you know that? The smaller you are, the quicker your heart beats. But it doesn't matter what size your heart is, we all only get an average of about two billion beats over our lifetime. It's just a pump at the end of the day, right? And all these pumps, they give up after two billion beats. That's why littler animals don't live as long. Their hearts have been beating faster the whole time so two billion beats comes a lot quicker for them.

ASHA. You're not that short.

BETTINA. I know.

ASHA. Like, you're short, but I don't think it's going to make that big a difference. Not so you'll notice. You know. When your time comes.

BETTINA. When I get on the bus, my heart beats so fast I swear everyone can hear it. Even the driver, behind the plastic screen. That's how loud it is. And then I get so embarrassed it beats harder. And faster. And that happens every day.

ASHA. It just feels like that.

BETTINA. What if it's not just my birthday money they're taking away? What if they're like... taking away my *life*.

ASHA. Fucking hell, Bettina, you don't have to be so dramatic all the time.

BETTINA. What if every time they pick on me it's shaving, I dunno, three days off the end for me? Like, three thousand beats or something.

ASHA. It's not that serious.

BETTINA. What if it is? Would you help me then?

ASHA. Didn't say I wouldn't help you.

BETTINA. You'll do it then?

ASHA. Look, far as I can see, you've got three options. One, do what they want, which you're already doing.

BETTINA. Sort of, yeah.

ASHA. Which you're *actually* doing, you're doing exactly what they want without so much as a peep. It's pathetic.

BETTINA. Alright. You don't have to be mean about it.

ASHA. Two, fight back.

BETTINA. That's what you'd do.

ASHA. I'd do *something*.

BETTINA. Except they wouldn't pick on you in the first place.

ASHA. They might have done... I mean, when I was in Year 10, they might have done.

BETTINA. So how did you stop being that kid?

ASHA. What kid?

BETTINA. A kid like me.

ASHA. ...You don't want to stop being *you*.

BETTINA. It's easy for you to say, you're not getting picked on every day.

ASHA. Why don't you do this to Steph and Milo? Argue with them until they lose the will to live?

BETTINA. If I annoy them I'll get slaps.

ASHA. So that leaves option three. Act like you're doing what they want, but really do what *you* want. Play the long game. Play it *smart*.

BETTINA. Is that what you're doing?

ASHA. What?

BETTINA (*re: the graffiti*). With Mrs L?

ASHA. It's not the same.

BETTINA. You're just doing what she wants, then?

ASHA....No.

BETTINA. They're taking my money for no reason. You're in the shit for no reason.

ASHA. That's a... false equivalence.

BETTINA. Mel Summers pushed in. She was asking for it.

ASHA. She didn't just... push in. She... dissed me.

BETTINA. What did she say?

ASHA (*direct address*). I'm thinking, how come Pankhurst is Mrs L's? And Gandhi and Ambedkar aren't? Because like... Mrs L's closer to them age-wise, isn't she? But she meant they're brown dudes... So is that how she sees me? Like, me being brown tops me being a girl? And do other people think that too? And then, all of a sudden, I get a shove in the middle of my back – sharp, right in my spine. And I realise the queue's moved on in front of me. And I hear Mel behind me. And she says, I swear, 'Get a move on, Paki.' And I don't even stop to think, I turn around and push her, both hands on her chest, bam!

BETTINA. Did she call you a bitch or something?

ASHA. What?

BETTINA. Is that why you pushed her?

ASHA....Yeah. Yeah, she did... (*Direct address*.) Don't tell her, okay? She doesn't need to know about this shit.

BETTINA. Serves her right then, doesn't it?

ASHA. Mrs L was all 'I'm really disappointed in you, Asha', and 'I'm really not sure you've considered how actions like this could impact upon your future.'

BETTINA. She knows there must have been a reason, yeah? Like, you're not the kind of person who's going to lash out like some sort of animal? Right?

ASHA (*direct address*). And I wasn't quite sure what she meant at first. Like, what's she saying? I'm not going Goldsmiths because I pushed Mel Summers over in the common room? Mel's making out she's, like, sustained serious injuries or something. And Mrs L's taken the bait. Says I need to learn to control my temper. Says I should know better than to resort to violence. I tell her there're some things that shouldn't be tolerated. The P-word being one of those things. So she makes a big deal out of getting Mel to apologise. But it was bare obvious Mel didn't mean it. It was just to make Mrs L feel better.

BETTINA. I'll go with option three, Asha. Tell me what to do.

ASHA. I'm not telling you what to do.

BETTINA. Sounds like the only way to avoid getting slaps and actually winning.

ASHA. You're not going to win anything.

BETTINA. Keeping my pocket money's winning.

ASHA (*direct address*). And now I'm here thinking, hold up. I'm cleaning their property for them, for free...? What the actual fuck...? And yeah I got eighty per cent on my paper, but Mrs L didn't even get what I was saying in it, so does that actually mean anything? And I'm thinking, what should Ambedkar have done? Because he knew he was right. He knew Gandhi was playing him. But what could he have done…? To win, I mean… (*To* BETTINA.) You need to snitch on them. Tell the driver.

BETTINA. The driver knows. He just pretends not to notice.

ASHA. Then… tell him they're doing something worse. Tell him one of them's pulled a knife on you.

BETTINA. What? I can't do that.

ASHA. He has to stop the bus then. He has to lock the doors, and call the police.

BETTINA. Right, and how long'll it take for them to turn up? Everyone'll be late. They'll all hate me. And then they'll find out I'm a liar.

ASHA. So?

BETTINA. …*That's* option three…?

ASHA (*direct address*). And Mrs L tries to make out Mel's being taught a lesson because she's cleaning the gates at the Stephen's Road entrance. Except how is that teaching Mel a lesson if I'm being made to do exactly the same thing? (*To* BETTINA.) Tell everyone you've been collecting money for charity for weeks and these fools are depriving little kids of breakfast vouchers or something.

BETTINA. Breakfast vouchers?

ASHA. Yeah. Or, I dunno. Abandoned donkeys.

BETTINA. Who abandons donkeys?

ASHA. Haven't you seen the collection boxes? They've got one in Costcutters.

BETTINA. Have they?

ASHA. Make a big thing about all the people who've donated. How much it was going to help. Tell everyone a load of donkeys are going to be put down now, or something.

BETTINA. …You think that'll work?

ASHA. It'll make them look bad. No way they're going to try to take your money in front of everyone then.

BETTINA. It's a lie though.

ASHA. …Yes.

BETTINA. What if they find out?

ASHA. Who?

BETTINA. Steph and Milo and that lot.

ASHA. Who cares? Only matters what the people on the bus think. Get them onside and Steph and Milo are screwed.

BETTINA. Isn't that bad, though…? Like… Wouldn't that make me as bad as them, sort of thing?

ASHA. No. It's self-defence, isn't it? Only defence you've got.

BETTINA. That's not true.

ASHA. Right. You're going to bust out some ju-jitsu moves I've never seen then?

BETTINA. Thought you were going to tell me how to outwit them.

ASHA. I did.

BETTINA. Lying and getting everyone to feel sorry for me isn't outwitting them. Doesn't this make me look, like… even more pathetic?

ASHA. Instead of your genius plan to get your big sister to beat them up for you?

BETTINA. I only asked. Didn't know you were so embarrassed of me.

ASHA. I'm not.

BETTINA. Ashamed.

ASHA. Listen up, you're not a little kid any more. It's about time you realised the system is *rigged*.

BETTINA. What system?

ASHA (*direct address*). Went to the staffroom to find Mrs L. Hadn't exactly worked out what I wanted to say, but I had a feeling if I could just explain about my essay... How she'd got it wrong. Got *me* wrong. I could make her see it wasn't fair to send me out here – (*Re: the cleaning brush, etc.*) to do this. When I got there the door was open and I could see Mrs L talking to Mr Hodgeson. They were laughing, and she was showing him something in one of those fancy Tupperware boxes.

BETTINA. The ones with the clips?

> ASHA *snaps out of her reverie, stunned* BETTINA *can hear her thoughts.*

ASHA....What?

BETTINA. One of those metal ones?

ASHA....Yeah...

BETTINA. Did she see you?

ASHA....Hodgeson did.

BETTINA. Mrs Ahmed was poorly last week so he took over our class for chemistry, and he let off the *biggest* trump when he was reaching up to wipe the board. It was *gross*.

> BETTINA *chuckles at the memory.* ASHA *just looks at her with fresh eyes.*

> What did you say to Mrs L?

ASHA. I...

BETTINA. Did you put her right?

ASHA. Hey?

BETTINA. Mrs L. In the staffroom?

ASHA. No... I sort of smiled and waved. He asked if it was important – they were on their lunch break. Then her phone rang and she went off to talk by the window. I hung around for a few minutes, but I started to feel stupid, so I left.

BETTINA. I'll go see her first thing if you like? Imagine Mum found out about Mel Summers. No way she'd stand for someone talking to you like that. They'd both be *dead*.

ASHA. You don't have to that.

BETTINA. I don't mind.

ASHA. No, really – don't do that, okay?

BETTINA. Alright.

Beat.

ASHA. I'm still not beating anyone up for you.

BETTINA. I know.

BETTINA *offers* ASHA *a crisp. This time she takes one.*

(*Re: the graffiti.*) Is it live, or live?

ASHA. How should I know?

BETTINA. You really didn't do it?

ASHA. I wouldn't have been stupid enough to tag my own name on the college gates.

BETTINA. Yeah, they wouldn't know though, would they? What your name means.

ASHA. *A*live. My name means *a*live.

BETTINA. It'd be a good tag for you.

ASHA. I don't need a tag.

BETTINA. I'm just saying. It'd work. If you wanted one… There's the bus.

ASHA *quickly starts to pack up her things, and put on her jacket.*

You finished, then?

ASHA. No. But I am done.

BETTINA. Still walking?

ASHA. I'll come with you.

ASHA *and* BETTINA *walk over to the bus stop together.*

The End.

The Kiss

Zoe Cooper

Character

LOU, *female, thirty-eight*

Words in [square brackets] are intention, and not to be spoken.

i.

Two beady eyes stare up.
He snuffles his nose and does a little – (*Squeaks*.)
And in this moment I think that if I squeeze too tight he will
just.

It's horrible that thought, isn't it?
Arriving uninvited and.
The same thought or,
maybe,
is instinct a better…?
When standing on platform three at Haymarket station as the
Metro to Gateshead comes speeding out of the tunnel on a wet
Wednesday afternoon.

The same sensation that shoots up through your legs.

I'm sure there is a German word for that.
That…
to jump or squeeze or.

But before we get to that.

ii.

Because back in the early days, just after we moved in,
at that point in the year when it was getting dark by four p.m.
which meant that I could see,
over the hedges and across the frozen lawns
into glowed-up windows.
Like the doors of an advent calendar.

A different scene presented just for me behind each one.
And I looked forward to this part of my day;
my-post-work-press-the-bell-on-the-bus-a-stop-early-so-that-I-
could-walk-through-our-new-estate-and-peep-in-at-other-
people's-houses.

A bald man in light-up reindeer jumper with teenager daughters,
chuckling together at something on the telly.
The very pregnant girl with a small unobtrusive silver cross
around her neck
and fashionably bearded husband –
who are decorating their tastefully restrained Scandi-inspired
tree
(the pair bought their house on the corner at the same time as us
and always make a point of waving rather demonstrably when
they see me and my wife out and about).
And the lopsided spruce with chocolate Santas and large paper
snowflakes coloured in with childish scribbles, at number seven
which signals I am nearly home.

And this particular night,
stood on our doorstep,
the woman from number seven.
She of the lopsided tree
talking to my Soph,
and holding a plastic kid's plate with two quite solid-looking
brownies on it.
And a card which reads 'welcome to your new home'.
Our complete address including postcode, underneath
in best joined-up handwriting.
And quite a good picture of a manatee
Which are his favourite animal
Mhairi
(*it's Scottish for Marie, though I hardly sound it these days*)
is explaining,
indicating a small person
clinging to her leg in an elf tunic which is really a dress
and jewelled slippers on feet,
the sort that very small girls wear at weddings
when they are being flower girls.

And there was something very deliberate about the whole
gesture of the visit that night.
She lingered for longer than she needed,
wanting, I think, for the neighbours behind those windows
which frame the dumbshow of nuclear family life so well,
to see her.
And for little Sammy in that dress and wedding slippers
(whose feet must have been cold, but who didn't seem to mind)
...to remember this moment.

iii.

Four months later.
Week three.
Is that right?
Or week four of the first lockdown.
and I have taken to standing in the window,
in the back bedroom,
at around this time every day
and so I am in my normal spot on a Thursday afternoon.

Their older boy, Ben,
is having a conversation with little Sammy in their back
garden.
Ben wants to play football,
but Sammy is holding a long skipping rope.
Of course you really need three to jump rope,
and I think Ben is trying to explain this
in the way that older siblings do have to.

Sammy does not respond,
just proffers the rope.

And in a clear escalation
Ben counter-offers the ball.
Arms rigid.
Jaw locked.

Annoyed at Sammy's silliness over the rope and more than that,
angry now too I think
because his birthright as firstborn is to choose what to play at.
I know this
because I too am firstborn
and I would not have stood for any such
insubordination
amongst my sisters.

In an unexpected show of defiance
Sammy bats the ball
out of Ben's hands.

They are both appealing
back to the house now
to the normal referee:
Mam Mam
they mewl.
But I have noticed that Mhairi doesn't get involved in these
sorts of disagreements.

Of course,
from up here I can see it all
as well as thinking I can hear it,
I check with Soph later though,
and she heard it too.
The next bit.

Over a row
of neat privet hedge
and three rather unruly leylandii
across two gardens
and through solid red-brick walls
with double glazing
past twisted tomato plants rising up from yogurt pots.

The thump as ball hit small boy flesh and bone.

The delay.

How when you are little
and something hurts you,

and it takes a moment
to register.

Then the scream.

The back door slamming.

I stare down
at little Sammy
staring at the ball.
The way that kids do when they have been frightened by their
own strength.

In this case their own ability to smash a ball directly into their
big brother's head.

And Sammy suddenly turns
and looks up.
Squinting against the low spring light.

I step behind a purple curtain
with flock flower motif
that we have still not got round to replacing.
Not sure why I am hiding.

iv.

The Sunday
after the Thursday
of the football incident in
let's just say it was week four
and Mhairi is on our front step again.
Well,
standing back from,
the way we are all meant to now,
in the scrubby bit of grass
that we have at the front,

amongst the dandelions
up around her ankles.

She looks about:
I pull them up by the roots, don't I, Sammy?
Sammy doesn't respond,
continues instead to cling to her leg and eventually
stoppers thumb in mouth.
Defiantly uncommunicative in highlighter-orange shorts and
pink T-shirt.

Because
I know it is tempting
to keep them when they are like this,
yellow and waving in the breeze.
But if you leave them like that
they will go to seed
and the wind will blow
and before you know it
the whole street.
And people are weird about that sort of thing round here…

She adds, sotto voce:

…especially – (Indicating.)
They basically accused us of being super-spreaders
when we first moved in.
Because Sammy likes to pick them
don't you, Sam?

Super-spreader.
Bit loaded now.

Sammy smiles shyly.
Unstoppers:
Cos of the virus.

And Mhairi puffs out her cheeks,
a pantomime of the dandelion-hating Mr Fallowfield
at number nine,
the house sandwiched between hers and ours.

Sammy giggles
at this bit of silliness.
Soph laughs,
she likes Mhairi
has been lobbying since those first brownies,
on that plastic kid's plate which we never got round to returning
for us to be,
not friends,
not exactly,
but friendly at least.

But I'm not,
despite the rainbow welcoming committee
there is something a bit too…
keen.

Being from London I am a bit,
I tend not to trust keen,
even, or rather especially now,
here,
from these people.
The kind of people who live round here.

And this has been difficult,
and it has frustrated Soph who is, herself, when we first met I
did think she was a bit.

Keen.

Anyway, I just thought I would pop round,
pop round to see how you are getting on.
I suppose you are still going in, Sophie?

Soph works at Cragside,
a primary school a few streets away
which was the other reason we moved,
why I was persuaded by Soph to move up the hill
to this area that calls itself High Heaton
allying itself to the more urban, more cosmopolitan Heaton,
but is really,
if you get in a taxi

you have to say Cochrane Park after the park the estate was
built over.
Otherwise the driver doesn't know what you are talking about.

Soph smiles a tired smile
in answer to Mhairi's question:
Keeps me busy.

Which is.

In class 3B Soph has five keyworker kids
who still come in,
as well as three 'at risk'
who live in a temporary housing block
for refugees who the council have not yet got round to
housing
who are meant to come in but haven't.
Haven't come in since the beginning of all this,
which makes Soph grey with worry some mornings.
She thinks I can't tell under her tinted moisturiser and keenness
but I do.
I can tell.

Keeps me out of trouble
She repeats again now,
trying I think to convince herself
as much as us.

And we've not seen you out and about much, Lou,
since the café closed.
Not that we have been –

I cut Mhairi off

Spying?

And why did I say that?

Sorry, Mhairi

And I can see Soph thinking this too as she repeats her apology
on my behalf:

Sorry, Mhairi, Louie…

Because it's very obviously me
who has been peeping at windows,
and twitching at curtains.

But Mhairi waves Soph's words away.

Anyway, the boys are finding it quite,
well,
like we all are...

...aren't we...

It's...

(Mhairi waits a beat, for LOU *or Soph to respond, which they*
don't...)

...I'm on nights,
and Evan is working from home,
and all on top of each other,
so the back garden has become contested land.
Well, I'm sure you heard.

I can't help but snort at this and say before I have given myself
time to think:

You've got a good kicking leg there, mate.

Mhairi and Soph stare.
This was the wrong thing to say.
Again.
But Sammy is smiling shyly at me
and so I do do a little wink back.

And we were wondering
because the front is a bit full with the car
and the boys' bikes.
The trampoline.
Which as you can imagine
has not been a welcome addition for some of our neighbours.

She glances over at number nine again.
Michael Fallowfield's concrete drive and giant concrete urn.
And I think she might know that the Fallowfields,

unlike those demonstrative evangelicals on the corner
don't feel that it is necessary to mask their prejudices,
but have instead kept up a steady stream of small complaints
about various things in the months since we moved in:
The speed of our wheelie-bin retrieval after bin day.
The noises of new-house DIY.
The height of one of the trees in the back garden which we
obviously inherited from the previous owners and which they
presumably tolerated for the entire period of their occupation of
the property.
And on one occasion,
before the world turned upside down
the sound of our 'laughter' one evening.
Coming from our bedroom.
Necessitating Mrs Fallowfield's move from the marital bed to
the indignities of the spare bedroom.
All of which have implied very effectively,
but in a way you can't quite put your finger on
that they do not welcome our presence.
People like us.
Soph manages to shrug these encounters off.
But the thing is.
With her shiny bob
And her tinted mosturiser like I said in zero one alabaster
And her general air of keenness
which mean that this sort of thing happens less to her
people like her
and when they do she is less.
So she thinks I am just being.

But I am dragged back from dwelling on that.
All that.
Again.
Because Mhairi's speaking:

*Anyway, all this means there is nowhere in the front
for us to put Ernie.*

(As herself.) Ernie?

Sammy stares at me.
All traces of that shy smile gone.
Back to sullen and sulky.
As if being made to share a favourite toy:

My guinea pig.

And we were wondering...

But Sammy cuts her off:

I wasn't.

If we could maybe, two birds with one stone I suppose.
Because Ernie likes dandelions doesn't he, Sam,
and you could come round every day,
any time you want, Sammy,
I'm sure the girls won't mind you popping round
to look after him and take him in at night.

And I am thinking that I might mind actually.
I might not want a seven-year-old on my front lawn,
staring in whenever he fancies.
Watching what I am doing.
Which I realise might sound a bit hypocritical but.

And he could eat up some of your long grass
and be safe from the terrible two.
And flying balls.

v.

The list was Soph's idea.
After she came back from work one evening in week eleven or
twelve and found me still in my sports bra and boxers at three
forty-five p.m.
Eating a peach yogurt over the sink.
It is a list of ten things I want to get done.
Well, ten things she wants me to want to get done.

Things that she hopes will distract me and also incidentally which she has wanted done for a while and which I have failed to do:

- One: Get dressed.

- Two: Leave the house once a day for a walk. Amended after my complaints that this was too ambitious to at least once every couple of days.

- Three: Paint downstairs toilet.

- Four: <u>Walk</u> (this second walk is underlined) to Wilkos to buy curtain hooks for the new curtains.

- Five: Join the Newcastle Black Lives Matter WhatsApp group which she is already an enthusiastic member of, ahead of the protest she is planning to go to at Monument on Saturday. Which I said I would. But. When I think about it, think about it and all those well-meaning people like Soph in that group who are organising the event up here I just feel so.

- Six: Ring my mother, her parents, my sisters for a chat and to set up a Zoom call for the weekend. She wants us to do a quiz.

- Seven: Phone the food bank to find out about the progress of my application to volunteer there. They say they are full but Soph is suspicious about this and thinks that they or I or possibly both may be fibbing and that I just need to keep up a steady flow of keen requests. I have tried to explain that the food bank is a charity doing important work in very difficult circumstances and probably a slightly bored café-manager-slash-singer-songwriter whose wife thinks she is eating too much yogurt is not their top priority. She is unmoved by this argument.

- Eight: My guitar which I've not picked up since the café closed. Which Soph finds particularly baffling as I've all the time in the world now to write songs. Songs about I don't know what, since I never go anywhere or do anything any more.

- Nine: Get my tax return out of the way. (I am not sure how I
  will be cheered by this but as I say, she sees this pandemic as
  an excellent opportunity to get all the things she has wanted
  sorted sorted so that I will have more time for the new list
  she has started covertly composing for after the pandemic,
  once I have solved systemic racism, put a stop to childhood
  poverty and completed said tax return.)

- Ten: Set up a Facebook group for my team at the café. I have
  got as far as logging in and typing in a series of suitably droll
  group names but when it comes to clicking the 'publish
  page' button I just.

- And scrawled at the bottom, a late entry after reading about
  the mood-boosting properties of gardening in her
  mindfulness magazine: Plants. Seeds. The growing of.

And at least with that last one I have made some progress.
I started lining up my yogurt pots
along the windowsill
in our bedroom in week one
and since then, as I have eaten more yogurts
I have been able to add to my collection.
Every window is now occupied
I am doing tomatoes
runner beans
and strawberries.
I am growing herbs.

Every morning I get up with Soph
and I go downstairs with her.
I diligently pinch out sideshoots on my tomatoes,
restake my runners with the free chopsticks we would get
before I was furloughed, lost all my gig bookings
and we decided that we actually preferred the inexpensive
meals we now make with lentils or
chickpeas pepped up with ancient herbs from the back of our
cupboard anyway.

I do all this while she eats breakfast.
Wave her off as I water carefully.

Before slumping back onto the sofa
the minute she has rounded the corner
for another day of working my way through the entire back catalogue
of *The Great British Bake Off*.
And eating dairy products.
And spying.
Only this morning,
the morning of The Incident, I have slept in.
Because last night I couldn't sleep.
Tossing and flailing and at one point apparently sitting bolt upright and shouting
before Soph managed to make me lie back down.
So I have slept, she has allowed me to sleep in past her six-fifteen alarm.
Her idea of a treat.

vi.

I come down the stairs at one thirty-two.
Into the front room to do my morning rounds,
which are now my afternoon rounds,
and in this moment I remember that I.

Because last night it was hot
and we had the windows open
and I meant to close them before we went to bed.
But after we got the call.

The call from the clinic that we had been expecting of course
since the beginning of lockdown
when it was announced that all non-urgent operations
and in our case I suppose 'non-essential' treatment
would be cancelled.
And I drank three glasses of wine.
Because what had been the point,

what was the fucking point
in the vitamins
and the keeping track of our cycles on three different apps
and the avoiding caffeine
and the not drinking anything for the last six months
now that it wasn't going ahead.

As Soph frowned at me from her slumped position on the sofa
I sloppily poured my fourth glass
and told her I was *fine, just fine*.
And to please stop staring.

But now the sill is wet.
On the floor scattered
three of the tomatoes.
One which had.
Was the only one that had fruit.
Snapped at the stem.
And I feel.
Or rather I don't feel, didn't feel anything as I picked them up.
Through the front door to the recycling.

And I realise that this is the first time I have set foot outside for.
The damp bricks on the drive against the slap of the bare soles
of my feet.
I am closing the garden waste bin that Soph ordered for us
after I said I would
but didn't.
Kept forgetting to, along with everything else.

When I feel eyes on me.
I turn and we lock, him watching me, watching him
as he slowly munches a dandelion.
Stem first all the way up to the yellow flower.

vii.

Why are you wet?

Soph's face looms over.

Why are you wet and why are you lying on the bathroom floor and why.

Well, part of her face.

Jesus.

I can only really see her forehead.

Your face, Louie!

Her forehead and her hairline.

What have you done to your face?

Because my eyes.

Your eyes are.

I had a shower
I try to say but it comes out all wheezy.

Because I was feeling a bit.
I was throwing away the tomatoes because they snapped, Soph,
in the storm last night and –

It's not.
That is not.
I don't think that tomatoes have.
Could have.

I meant to close the window when we went up to bed but I
I had that wine after they called
And so when we went to bed I must have forgotten
And so the tomatoes had.
They had.
Three of them snapped in the storm.

My chest is tight
and I can't seem to get enough air in.

So I put them in the brown bin
but I think I must have.
The smell was so strong,
like my granddad's lean-to,
my fingers were bright green when I washed them in the sink.
And that is when I started itching,
so I thought I should have a shower,
wash it off but.

I'm ringing…

No, don't, I'm
I'm,
it's just a bit of a…

But she is unpocketing her phone already.

They're busy enough as it is, Soph

Unlocks and dials.

I mean they made that very clear when they rang us –
Urgent care only they said.
And this is hardly…

Hello?

I stagger up unsteadily,

No, my wife.

As she turns slightly from me
And is rattled through the usual questions:

No, no
Or a high temperature.
No.
It's not.
No of course you have to ask, of course.
Sorry.

And she does sound.

I'm not normally…

She is never normally short with people like this.

…sorry, sorry…

Normally annoyingly.
So she must be.

As I sway in front of her,
imploring her with my eyes.
Well, eye.
To.
Stop.

Put the phone down.

No blood.
No.
She's thirty-eight.
She's conscious but she was out cold when I got home.
Passed out on the floor of the bathroom.
No.
No.

She gets a bit down sometimes, but…

She glances sort of at me, not at me.
Sort of asking for permission,
but also that look she gets
when she has already decided what the best thing is to do.

Seroxat, but she came off that for…
Because we were meant to be starting treatment for,
to start treatment, trying to have a.

I give her a look.

Baby.

Look, it's not that anyway.
We had some bad news about.
About that last night but this.
This isn't.
She hasn't taken anything.

A pause.
Ever so small.
But still.
An implied question.

I mouth
NO.
Of course I didn't.

Her face is.
One of her eyes is swollen shut,
and that side of her face
is much bigger than the other and her pupil,
the one that I can see.

She pulls back my hair and I smell her –
vanilla and sweat from a day of trying to keep
a clutch of seven-year-olds jolly when nothing is jolly
and I just want to go to sleep on her shoulder
but she is peering into my good eye.

And I know this sounds weird
but the white around her eye is swollen up around the pupil.

And as my legs begin give out under
I start to twist
I glimpse the bathroom mirror
a tight shiny face half-swollen
and then I feel a whooshing sensation and.

viii.

I am strapped down,
there is a man with arm tattoos writing on a clipboard.
I can't see his face.
He looks over at me.
Which is when I realise that I am making the noise.

That noise.
A sort of snuffling, squeaking sort of.

Decided to join us then?

I don't say anything
because I am distracted by the siren that has suddenly started to
sound.
And the jangling metal inside the van as we speed up.

Gaz will just have switched them on because we hit traffic.
Gaz hates traffic.
Nothing to worry about.
Your wife is lovely, isn't she?
I'm afraid we had to leave her at home.
Rules at the moment, you know?

I nod, dully.
I know.

We've had to give you some adrenalin
just as a precaution
but you'll be fine.
It was an allergic reaction to something.
Your wife said you'd no idea what it could've been?

And in this moment I take a big gulping gasp in
and I can feel the tears starting to roll unevenly
down my big swollen face.

I kissed him –

What?

And I don't.
I realise in this moment how much I don't want to admit this,
all this that has happened
and also how much I want to tell someone.

I saw him staring up at me
through the wire mesh of his run
and so I went
to pick him up.
Just to hold his hot little body in my hand.

Just to feel a tiny heartbeat against my fingers and I just.
I don't know why I did it,
I don't know what made me,
an instinct I suppose.
In that [moment]
to bend down and kiss him.
Right on top of his tiny head.

I say all this, gulping down big gasps of air.
And then I pass out again.

ix.

Iris Brickfield Community Park
is not the sort of park anyone makes a special visit to,
it's not even the sort of park you would walk to
if it was more than twenty minutes away.
It is a very average sort of park,
with a very average sort of playground
built on patchy asphalt,
a nature pond
planted quite generously with reeds
but also with at least twenty tinnies floating in it.
And a series of poems by a local poet mounted on wooden
poles
spaced out along an unconvincing 'nature path'
and always, always a hunch of teenagers
strategically positioned in their hoodies
on the only good benches.

But it is in fact not twenty minutes from our house, it is only ten
and since last summer when my snogging that guinea pig
did cause me to go into anaphylactic shock,
and spend a couple of embarrassing days in hospital,
wasting valuable NHS resources and feeling very guilty about it
I have taken to coming here most days,

sometimes on my own or more often,
like today,
with Mhairi and.

Sammi
(the 'y' of that name exchanged for an 'i' now
and sometimes practised in full as Samantha)
is picking floppy crocus and still-green daffodils while their
brother runs laps.
And Mhairi is telling me in hushed tones that the school have
been supportive,
Sammi's friends have mostly been okay about it and their
brother is coming to terms with it.

Sammi appears at our side and Mhairi breaks off what she is
saying.
Sammi is holding a bouquet of the floppiest crocus
and Mhairi is trying to adjust her face from crumpled and
concerned
to not worried at all,
about how to raise this little person who she thought was a little
boy,
but who we all think now might turn out to be a little girl.

And as I fix the crocus in my buttonhole
I think about the letter burning a hole in my pocket
that arrived as I was leaving just now.
Offering for us to start that previously abandoned treatment
that we can now barely afford
and which, when I think about it sometimes feels like it belongs
to another time,
to another us before everything changed.

And we all three sit down on the normally occupied
but now miraculously available bench
and I think I didn't need the coat I am wearing,
shrugging it off my shoulders and feeling the sun on my neck.

They rest their head against my shoulder
watching their brother sulkily,
thumb in mouth.

And I think that me and Soph.
When she gets back from school later we need to have the chat,
that chat we have both not been having for some time now.
About what to do next.
Or perhaps what not to do.

And I listen to the sound of a woodpigeon
who I have learnt to recognise
singing from their unlikely nest –
a few twigs and a piece of twine in a nearby hedge.
And I feel.

The End.

Prodigal

Kalungi Ssebandeke

Characters

RITA, *twenty-six, black*
KASUJJA, *thirty, black*

Present day. A winter morning on a council estate.

RITA *places her shopping down to open the front door. From the side emerges* KASUJJA. *He's dressed in funeral garb.*

KASUJJA (*singing*). 'We're supposed to be family, living together in harmony but we fight and we struggle.'

Need a hand?

RITA. You're a little late.

KASUJJA. Better late than never.

RITA. I would have preferred the never.

KASUJJA. Come on, Rita, don't be like that. She was my mother too.

RITA. Good to know you remember.

KASUJJA. I bought a suit and everything.

He does a little spin for her. She stifles a smile.

RITA. It's a nice suit. Looks expensive.

KASUJJA. Thought I'd beg borrow or steal so I can look good for Mum.

RITA. How much?

KASUJJA. What?

RITA. I'm sure whoever you begged, borrowed or stole from needs their money back. So how much?

KASUJJA. You think I'm here to ask my little sister for money?

RITA. Why else would you be here? The funeral was last week.

KASUJJA. I know. I just… Look, let's talk about this inside.

RITA. I really don't have time for this, Kasujja. I've got so many things to sort out before –

She stops herself.

KASUJJA. Before what?

RITA. It's none of your business.

KASUJJA. What are you up to, Rita?

She reluctantly tells him.

RITA. I'm selling the flat.

KASUJJA. Over my dead body.

RITA. No, over Mum's dead body.

KASUJJA. Are you being serious?

RITA. Yes. It's what she wanted.

KASUJJA. No, what Mum wanted was for us to have somewhere to call home.

RITA. What do you know about what she wanted? You've been gone for five years and haven't called once.

KASUJJA. You don't understand.

RITA. Why don't you help me understand, Kasujja? Help me understand why you missed your own mother's funeral.

KASUJJA. I missed Dad's. That didn't bother you too much.

RITA. Yes because I understood why you may not be there for that one. I mean after all he wasn't there for us. But *Mum's* funeral? Really?

KASUJJA. Let's talk about this inside.

RITA. Na, let's do this out here.

He pauses.

KASUJJA. How's Lawrence, Rose and Fred?

RITA. Broken, Grieving, Annoying.

KASUJJA. Okay.

You look great. Twenty-five looks good on you. You look more grown up.

RITA. The ageing process doing its job. Great observation. You came all the way from Lord knows where to point out the obvious?

KASUJJA. I didn't see you making an effort.

RITA. Effort for what?

KASUJJA. To get me and Mum talking again.

RITA. What was I to do? Force you two? You're both as stubborn as each other.

KASUJJA. But she was the mother. She was supposed to be the bigger person.

RITA. Speaking ill of the dead.

KASUJJA. Sorry.

A pause.

RITA. Look, I don't have time for this.

KASUJJA. I'm trying.

RITA. You're not trying hard enough.

KASUJJA. You know what? What's your problem with me?

RITA. I'll tell you my problem. You think the world revolves around you but guess what? It don't.

KASUJJA. Say how you really feel.

RITA. And you wanna know something else? I'm glad you didn't come to her funeral. Because if you had, everyone would've been on pins and needles.

KASUJJA. Do *you* wanna know something else? Growing up in there, you all made me feel ugly. It's like because I was born in Uganda you all thought I was Third World. So yeah, of course I wasn't gonna turn up.

RITA. What has that got to do with Mum? She fucking adored you.

KASUJJA. Then why did she leave me?

She could've brought me to London with her but she took Lawrence and left me.

RITA. That's the reason you didn't come to her funeral? Because she 'left' you? What did you want her to do? Leave her newborn with some strangers and bring you?

KASUJJA. She could've stayed. Instead *I* was left with the strangers while you all played happy family.

RITA. You joined us eventually.

KASUJJA. Do you have any idea how it feels for a ten-year-old to step into a ready-made family?

RITA. No I don't. But I do know how it feels to go through twenty-one years of punishment for something you had nothing to do with.

KASUJJA *pauses briefly. Maybe she's right.*

KASUJJA. Now you see why I didn't come? Having to ruin her funeral with us bickering. Going back and forth about who did what. I understand you don't want to see me but I need to get something from Mum's room.

RITA. You're not going anywhere near her room.

KASUJJA. You don't understand.

RITA. No, *you* don't understand. You're not stepping foot inside there.

KASUJJA. Mum gave me very clear instructions about what would happen after she died.

RITA. Funny, 'cause I spent her last moments with her and she didn't mention that to me.

KASUJJA. Maybe because she didn't trust you.

RITA. Mum trusted me.

KASUJJA. But she didn't trust you with her money.

Pause.

She didn't tell you, did she?

RITA. Her pension has been sorted out.

KASUJJA. Not the pension. Her life insurance.

RITA. You're lying.

KASUJJA. Let me in and find out.

RITA. They wouldn't insure her.

KASUJJA. She took it out before the diagnosis. And according to their policy summary, they will pay out if she dies – which has clearly happened; or if she is diagnosed as being terminally ill, and in the opinion of her hospital consultant and their medical officer, the illness is expected to lead to death within twelve months… which also happened. I guess you weren't as close as you thought.

RITA. How much?

KASUJJA. Fifty grand. Ten for each of us.

RITA. Do the others know?

KASUJJA. I was the only offspring she trusted. Said, I was most likely to be fair.

RITA. You, fair?

KASUJJA. Yeah. You see, unlike you – I don't think I'm king of the hill. I put everyone on equal footing, from, Lawrence all the way down to Fred.

RITA. But, I was there. For nearly a whole year I looked after her. All you did was get up and leave four years prior and even then she still chose you.

KASUJJA. Because she trusted me.

RITA. When did she tell you this?

KASUJJA. A week before I left.

RITA. But you didn't tell anyone you were leaving. You just got up and left.

KASUJJA. She must have sensed I was planning my escape. So when you were all out one day she bit the bullet, sat me down and told me the plan. It was long before she knew she was ill but it felt like the end.

RITA. Yeah 'cause you were about to fuck off for five years. And not once did you think to call her. Not even after her diagnosis?

KASUJJA. Well, I'm here, now. Just as she wanted.

RITA. Why do you need this... thing to make the claim? Can't you do that online?

KASUJJA. I need the policy number which will be on a pack they sent her when she took out the claim.

RITA. Tell me where it is. I'll get it for you.

KASUJJA. Are you serious? That's *my* home as well.

RITA. You haven't been here for all these years so technically it's not. As far I'm concerned you're a stranger trespassing.

KASUJJA. You know if I wanted to I could just push past you.

She approaches him. Face to face.

RITA. Why don't you try and see what happens.

A tense moment. He gives in.

KASUJJA. Bottom drawer of the main wardrobe, the yellow plastic bag. Oh and, Rita. I will need the death certificate too.

RITA *gets her shopping and steps in leaving him outside. He stands, takes out a spliff and starts smoking. He starts to play music from his phone, it's his own music. He dances around euphorically.*

RITA *returns with the yellow bag and a laminated death certificate. She watches him dance, he is oblivious to her watching him.*

RITA. Found it.

KASUJJA. Ah, yes! This is it. Thank you.

RITA (*before handing it to him*). When do we get ours?

KASUJJA (*distracted*). What?

RITA. Our share. When do we get it?

KASUJJA. Soon. I just gotta call the insurance company. Make the claim, then yeah we'll all get ours in about five days.

RITA. How much did you say?

KASUJJA. Thirty grand.

RITA. Fifty. You said fifty grand.

KASUJJA. Thirty, fifty, it's all the same. Just give me the bag.

RITA. You started again?

KASUJJA. Oh, this? Come on, this is nothing. It's weed.

RITA. You know how Mum felt about you and drugs.

KASUJJA. It's weed. Okay? You drink, right?

RITA. Yeah –

KASUJJA. Then what's wrong with me smoking?

You don't trust me, do you? You think, I'm gonna take this money and smoke it all away?

RITA. Well, are you?

KASUJJA. Yes, Rita. I'm gonna waste fifty grand on weed. Come on, don't be foolish. Just give me the bag.

She holds on to it.

Okay, now I'm getting a little… upset.

RITA. Is that what you call it?

KASUJJA. Yeah. You're wasting my time. So please can I have the bag?

RITA. Tell me why first?

KASUJJA. Look, Rita. No more games?

RITA. Tell me why you never came back.

KASUJJA. You really wanna know? Fine. Let me tell you why. Because I had set myself free, why would I come back to this prison? And it wasn't just her. It was you, Lawrence, Fred, Rose. All of you. You all made me feel like the odd one out. Like just because, I didn't grow up with you all that it meant I was less of a sibling. I wanted to be somewhere I could feel free, laugh, dance, sing, without you all mocking me. New and improved. And yeah, I could've called. FaceTimed, fucking Zoom, even Skype, but I just didn't. It started off as a few days. A break from you all, then a week went by and before long it was five years. I tried to pick up the phone even when I found out about Mum, but my body kept telling me that I was better off without you all. I couldn't bear the taunts, the abuse, the tension. I couldn't bear you all.

RITA. We weren't that bad.

KASUJJA. You were. Especially you.

RITA. Me?

KASUJJA. You were the ringleader. The Rachel McAdams.

You all went on holiday once and I chose to stay. It wasn't because I couldn't afford it. It was because I wanted to know how it felt to be alone in the flat.

Just me. And you know what, it felt great. I was silly, I was serious, I was calm, I was wild. I was everything you all never let me be. And one day when you were all still on your... family holiday, I brought a girl back and she immediately could sense a negative energy oozing from the flat.

RITA. Maybe it was coming from you.

KASUJJA. Oh, believe me, it was residue from you all.

RITA. I never knew.

KASUJJA. Of course you didn't.

RITA. But you had us all walking on eggshells. So if it felt like we were being negative it's because we were trying to navigate around your landmine of a temper.

KASUJJA. What are you on about?

RITA. I don't think you know this, Kasujja, but you have a rage. And whenever you let that out, Mum would let you get away with murder. When she wasn't trying to fix you she would think of all types of excuses during your spells. 'He never had me and your dad for such crucial years.' 'He's a man.' 'He's the eldest.' You were so broken. And it kept getting worse. From you changing your accent, your name and even your voice.

KASUJJA. If Mum fixed me then why would she decide to break *you*?

RITA. Because you were her special boy.

KASUJJA. If I was so special why did you all make me feel so odd? Is it a wonder I changed my accent? I wanted to fit in and be like you all. My name? Well that was never my name. I am a Muganda man and I should have a Buganda name. And as for my voice? I grew up. Stopped being a child and started being a man.

RITA. Is that what you think that is? If you were a man, you wouldn't be hiding from your family because we called you names or wouldn't let you sing. You would be brave enough to state your point without being aggressive.

You would be there for your dying mum, fuck, you would go to her funeral. But no. You decide to be a cartoon image of what a man is.

She throws him the bag.

So here, take the fucking bag. Divide it, smoke it, do whatever you want. I don't care. I'm done looking after people that don't appreciate me.

She's now broken. Possibly tearful. They stand in silence.

He looks at the yellow bag on the floor. He walks towards and spills the content on the floor. It's a photo album along with the insurance-claim paperwork.

He picks up the photo album. He looks through it and starts laughing.

What's so funny?

KASUJJA. These.

RITA. What is it?

KASUJJA. Photos. There are some of me as a baby, in Uganda.

RITA *walks towards him and stands next to him.*

RITA. I've never seen these before.

KASUJJA. Me neither.

RITA. Why did she have them hidden away?

KASUJJA. 'Cause Dad features in all of them.

RITA *picks out one.*

RITA. Except this one.

KASUJJA. Hahaha. This was the first time I met you all.

RITA. You look so happy.

KASUJJA. We all do. Oooh, except you in this one.

RITA. That's when I caught you drinking from my cup.

KASUJJA. I thought it was mine.

RITA. It was pink.

KASUJJA. Hey, I didn't subscribe to gendered societal trends.

RITA. Shut up. You couldn't even speak English.

KASUJJA. You see, that little six-year-old girl in this picture really thought I was some backward freshie.

RITA. Emphasis on six-year-old. You're not the only one who's changed.

KASUJJA. Yeah. You're right.

Wow. Mum played us. She played us well. She knew I was about to leave. So she made sure I would eventually be back.

RITA. And here you are. Back to collect your money.

KASUJJA. That's only half the reason. Yes, there have been some... debts. Starts out small, you know. You think, yeah I can pay that back. I got miracle money coming, I'm sure of it. But then you find yourself borrowing somewhere else to pay the first one and so on and so on.

RITA. You do know you could've called us. You didn't have to wait till Mum died.

KASUJJA. I know. But how would that look? Storm out then turn around and ask for help? Especially from the same family I pretty much abandoned. Rita, I really didn't mean to go for so long. I wanted to be my own man.

Stand on my own two feet.

RITA. But that's the beauty of having such a big family. There's always someone to lean on.

KASUJJA. That's it. No more Disney Plus for you.

RITA. Don't get it twisted, I'm still 'ard body.

They share a laugh.

What was the other reason?

KASUJJA. What?

RITA. You said the money was only half the reason you came back. What was the other one?

KASUJJA. You're really gonna make me say it?

RITA. Well, how else am I gonna know? I'm not a mind-reader.

KASUJJA. Rita, you know the reason.

RITA. I don't.

KASUJJA. Fine! It's 'cause I missed you. And not just you but the whole family, even Fred.

RITA. What? Did I hear that right? Stone-cold Kasujja missed his family?

She goes to scream out for the whole area to hear. He chases her trying to stop her.

DID YOU ALL HEAR THAT? KASUJJA MISSED HIS FAMILY!

KASUJJA. Shut up, before I take it back.

RITA. Sorry, too late. I'm sure even Mummy heard it.

They pause. A good vibe between them. Finally KASUJJA hugs his sister, who hugs him back.

He picks up the insurance documents, putting them back in the bag. He gives RITA the yellow bag but keeps the photo album.

You sort it.

RITA. You sure?

KASUJJA. Yeah. Maybe I can come back to help you clean the flat?

RITA. Maybe.

They smile as he turns to walk away, leaving her on the stage.

Alone, she sings:

'We're supposed to be family, living together in harmony 'cause we made it through struggle.'

The End.

Author Biographies

SONALI BHATTACHARYYA was 2018 Channel 4 writer-in-residence at the Orange Tree, where she wrote *Chasing Hares*, winner of the Sonia Friedman Production Award. Her credits include *Megaball* (Let's Play at National Theatre Learning), *Slummers* (Bunker Theatre), *2066* (Almeida Theatre), *The Invisible Boy* (Kiln Theatre) and *White Open Spaces* (Pentabus Theatre; South Bank Show Award-nominated). She was one of three playwrights selected for the inaugural Old Vic 12, and is currently under commission to Fifth Word and Kiln Theatre, writer-in-residence at the National Theatre Studio, and was recently shortlisted for the Woman's Playwriting Award for her play *Deepa the Saint*.

DEBORAH BRUCE's theatre credits include *The House They Grew Up In* (Chichester Festival Theatre), *The Distance* (Sheffield Theatres/Orange Tree Theatre; finalist for the Susan Smith Blackburn Prize), *Joanne* (Latitude Festival/Soho Theatre), *The Light* (Live Theatre), *Same* (National Theatre) and *Godchild* (Hampstead Theatre). As a director, her credits include *Pride and Prejudice* (Regent's Park Open Air Theatre).

ZOE COOPER's *Out of Water* had its world premiere at the Orange Tree in 2019 and was a finalist in the 2020 Susan Smith Blackburn Prize. She was also shortlisted for the Charles Wintour Award for Most Promising Playwright at the Evening Standard Awards 2019, and nominated for the Best New Production of a Play Award in the Broadway World UK Awards. Her playwriting credits include *Jess and Joe Forever* (Orange Tree Theatre/Traverse Theatre/UK tour; Off West End Award for Most Promising Playwright Award 2017, longlisted for the Evening Standard Most Promising Playwright Award), *Nativities* and *Utopia* (Live Theatre).

KALUNGI SSEBANDEKE was selected for the BBC
Writersroom London Voices, and Soho Theatre's Writers' Lab.
He was also selected for the Lyric Hammersmith ten-week
writers' programme and has written for the Young Vic, Bush
Theatre and Talawa. His credits include *Assata Taught Me* (Gate
Theatre). As an actor, his credits include *Blood Knot* (Orange
Tree Theatre).

JOEL TAN is a Singaporean playwright based in London. His
credits include *Love in the Time of the Ancients* (Shortlisted for
the 2019 Papatango Prize), *Tango* (Pangdemonium Theatre;
nominated for Life Theatre Award's Best Original Script), *Café*
(The Twenty-Something Theatre Festival), *The Actors Tour*
(international tour), *Mosaic* (M1 Festival) and *The Way We Go*
(Checkpoint Theatre). He is part of 503 Five, Theatre503's
residency scheme, and an associate artist with Chinese Arts
Now and Singapore's Checkpoint Theatre.

JOE WHITE's debut play *Mayfly* premiered at the Orange Tree
in 2018, for which he won Most Promising New Playwright at
the OffWestEnd Awards and was nominated for Best New
Writer at The Stage Awards. He has written work for the Old
Vic, Lyric Hammersmith, Bush Theatre, Hampstead Theatre,
Birmingham REP and BBC Radio 3. In 2014, he was selected
for the BBC Writersroom 10 and won the Channel 4
Playwriting Award. In 2015, he was the writer-in-residence at
Pentabus Theatre Company, and in 2017, he was selected for
the Orange Tree Writers Collective and the Old Vic 12. In 2019,
he was selected for the BBC TV Drama Writers Programme,
through which he is developing a pilot with STV. Joe is
currently under commission from the BBC, Sheffield Crucible,
Hampstead Theatre, Audible and Michael Harrison Productions.